LIVING WITH A PROPHETESS

LIVING WITH A PROPHETESS

Terry Atkinson

New Living Publishers
Manchester

First Published 2009

British Library Cataloguing in Publication Data
A catalogue record for this book is available
From the British Library

Scripture quotations are from the King James Version of the Bible,
unless otherwise stated.

Cover design by Roger Judd

ISBN 978-1-899721-12-2

Published in Great Britain by
NEW LIVING PUBLISHERS
164 Radcliffe New Road, Whitefield
Manchester M45 7TU England

Printed in Great Britain
by Cromwell Press, Trowbridge, Wiltshire

Contents

DEDICATION

There comes a time when God speaks, and our response to that voice determines what we think of the past, what we do in the present, and what we achieve in the future. Every time the Lord speaks it is to clear the way into a better, more perfect day, so that we might see Him clearly, love Him dearly, walk with Him nearly and serve Him consistently.

Terry Atkinson

All names have been changed.

ABOUT THE AUTHOR

Terry Atkinson, one of ten children, came to faith in Christ in Yorkshire, England, as a teenager. His early years in the ministry were spent founding churches in Perth, Western Australia. From Australia, Terry returned to England to study theology in Kenley, Surrey. He has been a minister of the gospel since the age of twenty-one, first pioneering a church in Gainsborough, Lincolnshire, England. He has been involved in Christian ministry for nearly fifty years, holding pastorates as far apart as Shrewsbury, Shropshire and Maryport in Cumbria. Now based in Manchester, England, he is at present engaged in itinerant ministry in the north-west of England and in Canada.

Terry is married to Margaret, whom he met while a theological student. She accompanies him during his ministry engagements, being used of the Lord to help and direct the lives of others who are in need. They have one daughter, two sons, and four grandchildren.

The author's writings cover many topics and include: *Dying Is Living* (on life after death); *In Sickness and in Health*; *The Growing Pains of Peter*, *Peter —the Mature Man* and *Diamonds in David* and *The Word of Knowledge in Action*.

1

THE FORMATIVE YEARS

It was a happy day when this child was brought into the world; it was the happiest of days, and the sunniest of hours, not to be cursed but to be blessed because a bundle of life was introduced to life and love. There was no cloud in the sky, and everything seemed rosy in the garden. These days belonged to the days of bright summer sun and long hours of sunshine. It was the best of times and the happiest of hours, yet just a few years before World War 2 with its bombs and devastation.

There was nothing to distinguish this birth from any other, yet it was sacred to the mother. On the outskirts of Wakefield, West Yorkshire, in the tiny village of Hall Green, a precious gift had been given: the gift of a child. A girl child was born, and the parents decided to name her Margaret, meaning 'pearl'. Not a solitary pearl would be seen in her life, yet a whole string of pearls would enhance her later life as she ministered for the

Lord. It would take many years to fabricate the chain on which these pearls would hang from. If ever there was a time that hope was born in a child, it was in this child, loved by mother, father, grandparents and everyone who entered that terraced house to gaze on her beautiful face. Everything had been carefully arranged in the home to make the child welcome. She was too young to read the word 'welcome' written on the doormat, but the preparation made by her parents spoke volumes. From the womb into the house did not seem a great transition, for there was deep love and acceptance in both. The stork that brought this child was called 'happiness' and 'cheer', for that would be the disposition of the child as she grew up. The photographs of Margaret at this age always revealed her with a bright smiling face, as if smiling was her only gift.

Silvanus Warwick, her father was employed by the National Coal Board, in the local mine. He became a 'shot firer' which meant that he had the authority to explode sticks of dynamite that had been put into a hole drilled into the coal, to blast the coal out of the seam. He was a man of keen sporting interest ranging from cricket to lawn tennis with football in between.

Bessie Warwick was employed as an insurance agent, work she did successfully for a number of years. As a visitor to many homes, people gladly confided in her, and she became an unpaid social worker. Both Margaret's parents had a keen business interest that was to be revealed in later years when they purchased their own self-service store, to which a Post Office was added. They named the business 'The Orchard Stores', and Margaret, with her two sisters, Gwen and Hilary, and brother, Chris, spent many happy days playing in the orchard situated at the rear of the premises.

In 1940 England declared war on Germany and from 1940 – 1945 an army camp was opened on Wooley Moor for internees, as prisoners of war. Margaret spent many happy days being cared for by a prisoner of war, carried around the village on the back of his motor cycle.

After spending her formative years in Hall Green, Margaret's parents decided to move to a small town called Ossett on the outskirts of Wakefield, West Yorkshire, close to where the hymn 'Onward Christian Soldiers' was written. Later the family moved to Wooley Moor, near to Hall Green on the perimeter of Wakefield, where they occupied a house which was part of a row built for the mining community. This house overlooked the moors, and it bred within Margaret a deep appreciation of the countryside, and all things wild and free.

Margaret loved to mix with the boys, because she felt she needed to be accepted by them. You could define her at this time as a 'tomboy'! She would wear shorts so that it seemed as if she was a boy. In her heart she wished she had been born a boy and not a girl! That had been born in her to equip her for the rigours of life that awaited her in the future, in pioneer work, and the difficulties she encountered in the 'ministry' for Jesus Christ. The schooling of God can take place in your own back garden or school playground.

In those days there were few buses, travelling was by foot from door to door. Margaret attended school in Painthorpe, Wakefield, West Yorkshire, England, a small village close to where she lived.

At eight years of age this young girl began to pray. Her prayers were simple and angelic. In the attic at home Margaret found a book with pictures of Divine healings, which interested her more than the 'comics' or 'girl' magazines of the day. As she read, a deep longing to know God was birthed in her. She would pray at the side of her bed 'Dear Lord, if you exist, please help me to know you.' It seemed as if there was a Divine hand on her life to guide and protect her for the years of usefulness that were before her.

Many days that begin with sunshine can end in clouds and storms. What had been a happy birth and early life was suddenly changed. The parents of this child were not very happy with each other. They were both strong willed. When arguing, Silvanus would shout so loud, and Bessie would turn her hearing aid down so she couldn't hear what he was saying, while she opened the windows so the neighbours could hear what kind of person she lived with. In later life they split up, living apart but they were never divorced. They came back together, and in the maturity of life they were most peaceful, because they both surrendered to Jesus Christ, and through the new birth, John 3:7, they experienced God's love for them, and that became their love for one another.

A local farmer favoured Margaret, and would take her on the back of his cart to deliver milk. It was here she found refuge and help from the many arguments between her parents. She was allowed to pour milk into the jugs that were left on the doorsteps of each house. This milk seemed to a young child as if it was purer than heaven, and whiter than the daisy in the farmer's field. When they were short of milk in the home, they always sent Margaret to the farm for a fresh supply. It was always a pleasure to bring back some of that so fresh and white as any freshly plucked daisy.

The years sped by as Margaret matured into a teenager, one child of a family of three girls and one boy. At thirteen years of age, a holiday was arranged for her with auntie Florence, the sister of Bessie Warwick. This auntie was a strong character, like a bull in a china shop! Bessie took Margaret on one side, and said, 'Be careful with auntie Florence and what she tells you, because she has 'religious mania'! Margaret didn't fully understand what her mother meant. 'Religious mania' might have been an illness like influenza as far as she was concerned! Bessie Warwick issued this dire warning against the influence of auntie Florence because Florence belonged to a local evangelical church, and was full of zeal because of her love for Jesus Christ. She was full of good works, and entertaining missionaries from abroad was her delight. One such missionary was Gladys Aylward, whose story was partially told in the film 'The Inn of the Sixth Happiness'.

Auntie Florence was a strong willed woman built like a steam train, and Margaret was to spend two weeks with her. If auntie Florence told you to do it, you did it without question. If she told you to go somewhere and you did not move, she would push you there! Florence was not a cruel woman but kind, with a will of steel and a voice to match!

During the holiday a party had been arranged for the Saturday evening, where a lot of young people would be gathering together. The thought crossed Margaret's mind that this would just be a time when they would play the usual games and there would be gifts of sweets, lots of cakes and 'yummy' jelly. After they had eaten, instead of the usual games, a meeting had been arranged by auntie Florence, and all were expected to go into that meeting. Margaret, when she heard that a local minister had been invited to speak, froze in horror. She had enough of that on a Sunday in the local church! Church was boring, the vicar was boring, even the vicar's cat was boring, she thought. Margaret stood outside the room prepared for the vicar and his congregation. Auntie Florence saw her hesitating, and asked why. Without receiving an answer she pushed Margaret into the room, declaring, 'All who come here must go in and listen to the minister!' Those words were as bands of steel around a young heart, and Margaret felt as if she had been imprisoned in Alcatraz.

Then, as the minister began to speak, it was as if a miracle happened. He was so different to the minister Margaret was used to hearing on a Sunday. He was bright and cheery. His personality filled the room, his face displayed his love for God, and his eyes sparkled with joy. He spoke as if he knew God as a friend, the words flowing from him. Margaret began to take notice. Her attention had been arrested. Her heart was as open as a book to what was being said. He spoke on 'Behold I stand at the door and knock, and if any man will hear my voice and open, I will come in and sup with him, and he with me.' What he said was better than sweets or cakes, jelly or trifle. It was what Margaret needed to hear at this moment in her life. When he made an appeal and explained how to receive Jesus Christ as Saviour, Margaret accepted those words as if her own mother was speaking to her. These words were as delightful as a new dress to a young child.

Bowing her head, she accepted Jesus as her Saviour. This was the beginning of an adventure that would take Margaret through both sunny and sour moments.

As Margaret prayed, it seemed as if she was being lifted out of her body. The joy was so immense; there was enough to fill a deep sea. God was giving her a vision, transporting her from earth to heaven. She could see and hear angels singing, yet in a language she did not understand. They were singing to Someone, with great joy and gladness. Margaret opened her eyes to find that she was back on earth, and had never left the room where she had been previously. She closed her eyes again, seeking to recapture the vision, but it was too late, it had disappeared. In later life Margaret realised that she had heard the angels singing over one sinner who had repented of her sins, Luke 15:7.

Margaret wanted to weep buckets and buckets of tears of repentance. When auntie Florence realised what had happened, and saw Margaret crying she told her she should be laughing and not crying because salvation was a thing of joy. As she left the house, looking up into the sky, the realisation gripped her spirit that God had made all that was seen in the sky at night and in the daytime. Margaret climbed into bed that night, and as the sheets covered her body, so she heard those angels singing again, as a heavenly choir, and they were singing as if they never would stop. She fell asleep soothed by angels singing.

Choruses and singing of them became the order of the day. When Margaret wanted to worship God she began to sing the choruses she had learned at the home of auntie Florence. There was depth, height, breadth and length as she learned of the love of God in her heart.

It was not long before all the family were told of her experience. To her it was so new, so real and so deep. Margaret thought when she told her family and those in the church about her experience in God they would be delighted. In the church she appealed to her own age group to believe on the Lord Jesus Christ, but they mocked her, and she could not understand how or why they could reject this wonderful thing that had happened to her. They would taunt her and say, 'Is God speaking to you now?'

Faithfully, this young disciple of Christ went to her own church every Sunday. As she entered the church, and as she left it, an inner voice pleaded constantly with her to tell those she met about Jesus Christ. The voice was compelling and impelling, as Margaret felt she must tell others about Jesus.

When Margaret was in the age-group between thirteen and fifteen years, you could be considered for Sunday school teaching, yet whenever she expressed her longing to teach she was denied. First one excuse then another was given. They did not want anyone who was claiming to be 'born again' to be teaching the children such things. It might be in the Bible but it was not in the church! The church was the authority over the Bible. The church alone could interpret the Bible.

Two weeks after her conversion, the inner voice of the Holy Spirit was still pleading with Margaret to tell them about Christ, but they would not listen. It all became too much for this little convert and she ran out of the church weeping, feeling sorrowful with a heart that had been broken by religious bigotry and formalism. The vicar and the Sunday school teachers followed her. The vicar took Margaret into the vestry. He wanted her to explain what had happened, and why all the fuss and tears. Margaret didn't know her Bible, for she was a new convert, a 'novice' meaning 'one newly planted'. She turned to John 3:7 and began to read to the vicar and the Sunday school teachers, emphasising what had happened to her was that she had been 'born again'. In John 3 it told about Nicodemus who needed to be 'born again', and Margaret thought that would explain how she felt. Through her tears she began to speak. The vicar said, 'I don't understand what you mean!' There was a metal cross on the front of his desk, so Margaret took hold of it, and she began to tell him of Jesus who died on the cross to forgive sins. The vicar patted Margaret on the head, and said, 'Go home, child, you are sick!'

He thought she was in need of a physician yet he himself was in need of the great Physician, Mark 2:17.

Margaret wept all the way home. If tears could have been turned into pearls, riches untold would have been hers. Each tear became an evangelist for the truth of the Bible.

When Margaret arrived home still crying, she told her mother, and said, 'Mother, they would not believe me!' As a mother would, Bessie flung her arms around her daughter to squeeze some comfort into her, and she said, 'I believe you! I believe you!' At that time she believed the story of Margaret, but it would take another fifty years before Bessie, Margaret's mother, would surrender her life to Jesus Christ. Bessie was prepared to believe it could happen to her daughter, but in the timing of truth she herself was not yet ready to make that commitment to Christ.

2

THE WILDERNESS YEARS

This new experience made Margaret different. The problem was that she did not know of anyone else with an identical experience; for a short time she thought she was the only person in the world to have had such an encounter with God. For two years she prayed that the Lord would lead her to those of like faith and convictions. She was as lonely and adrift as Jonah in the belly of the whale. She left the established church and began to spend Sundays at a local park with a friend.

Margaret's cousin, Freddy, had been invited to stay with the family for a holiday. Freddy was the adopted son of auntie Florence and uncle Albert Moss, who had been instrumental in leading Margaret to know Jesus Christ as her Saviour. He was a gifted pianist, and spent much time tinkling the ivories. One of the songs he played was 'The Old Rugged Cross', and one verse seemed to particularly speak to Margaret, 'To the old rugged Cross I will ever be true, its shame and reproach gladly bear.' Those words brought such conviction that they broke her into pieces. She felt that there had been a defining moment when she ran away from the minister who had a cross placed on his desk, and through it she had tried to explain what had happened to her. Margaret began to cry, and sobbing she prayed, 'Dear God, show me what You want me to do?' In her heart she was willing to go anywhere and say anything for Jesus Christ who had become her first love in life. At sixteen years of age she felt competent enough to make serious decisions about her future.

Conversion changed Margaret in every degree. As a youngster she had been so shy that if anyone came to visit the family she would retire to her bedroom, unable to face strangers, but now she had a new boldness, the boldness of a lion. The shyness was replaced with a shine.

On three consecutive nights Margaret dreamed the same dream. She saw herself standing in the traditional church pulpit that she had run away from. As she stood there, bold and resolute, she looked at the congregation, and to her amazement they looked like starving children, underfed, emaciated to the bone, with eyes standing out like door knobs, and skin hanging from every part of the body. Every bone could be seen and counted. All had a vacant stare, and were in a state of shock and remorse. Margaret heard a loud voice behind her, saying, 'Tell them about Me, tell them about Me, tell them about Me.' Then the voice added 'I am the Bread of Life.' Margaret began to testify of what had happened to her, to tell them of what the Lord had done in her life. Suddenly these seemingly underfed people began to develop muscles. Weakness became strength, and that which was withered began to mature.

Margaret felt that the Lord was directing her back to her own church, and with uncertainty as her companion she entered the building. Nothing had changed, the same architecture, the same minister, the same people, the same candles and ritual. Deep in her heart and on her lips was the desire to be a Sunday school teacher, but still they were very reluctant to let her teach the children this strange doctrine of being 'born again' of the Spirit of God. She was as odd to them as they were to her. There was no bridge to bridge the gap between both sides of the chasm existing between them.

Maureen, a Sunday school teacher, had her own class, and it was thought that if they sent Margaret with her, no harm would be done. Maureen's class were rude, rowdy and bawdy. They would make fun of Margaret, and she would become the stub of future jokes. Maureen conducted her class in the belfry! The idea was that this unruly class would wear themselves out climbing the many steps, and be too exhausted to cause trouble! Also they were so far removed in the belfry that no one would hear the awful noise they made. What should have been Bethlehem was bedlam. As Margaret walked behind Maureen, she was taken by surprise when Maureen, who did not really want to teach these rebels, said to her, 'I can see that you desperately want to teach a Sunday school class, why not teach my class?' They had nearly reached the top of the steps when Maureen added, 'As long as you do not tell the minister, everything will be fine.'

Margaret accepted the offer. She knew she would be in for a difficult time, for each child seemed to have a pirate and a parrot nature: they would not stop talking, and rebellion seemed to be their second name! She began to tell the children how and when God had changed her life by giving her new birth, making her a new creation. The effect was immediate, first one child and then another stopped acting the fool, and slowly began to sit down, showing an interest in what this pretty sixteen year old was telling them about Jesus. Interest grew into enthralment. They had never heard anything like this before. All eyes were riveted on the speaker, a thing never known before in the history of this class. The Holy Spirit began to move on young unregenerate hearts. Those things that had been spoiled and broken were being healed by an unseen Physician.

As Margaret finished speaking, and the holy

hush was still upon the children, Margaret decided through the promptings of the Spirit of God to make an appeal, and ask if anyone would like to accept Jesus as their Saviour. Each child, including the Sunday school teacher, repeated the prayer of repentance and acceptance. In the timing of God everything was beautiful, for as she finished the appeal, the bell rang, signifying the end of the teaching session for that day. Margaret knew there would be further rejection from the minister.

Margaret had a cousin named Barbara, who was a believer, although Margaret herself did not know much about that until one day Barbara asked if she would like to visit their church. At that time Margaret had no idea what different denominations believed or taught but, desperate for God, she would go anywhere and try anything. The hunger of a child was in her heart, and she must be fed. Her spirit could only be satisfied by the Spirit of the Lord. If only she could find others of like faith, people who believed the Lord as she did. Religion had left her dry and thirsty.

With these thoughts weighing heavily on her young mind and feeling like a fish out of water, Margaret began to walk up the steps that led into Barbara's church. As she approached the church the congregation was singing 'Jesus, Jesus, Jesus sweetest name I know, fills my every longing, keeps me singing as I go.' Suddenly there was an explosion of recognition within her heart; these people had the same faith that she had. Here were people that she loved already, just through hearing them sing although she had never seen them face to face. The feeling of the prodigal returning home overwhelmed her. None of the ornate columns of a traditional church were here, gone were the vestments and the pews; here were people sitting and singing as souls set free. She shouted the words within her soul, 'Home, sweet home!' The dove on the wing had come to rest on a branch of the vine. Margaret would be loved and accepted. Many years later, along with her husband Terry Atkinson, they would pastor this church.

Margaret was introduced to the minister of this Pentecostal church, R.J. Hayes, a gracious, kindly man who proved to be so helpful to this young convert. When she told him her story, he began to marvel at the grace of God that had kept her with little fellowship for over two years while she had been in the wilderness. That wilderness now blossomed as a rose.

A few months later, the same cousin Barbara invited Margaret to go on holiday with her to Scarborough Camp. This camp consisted of two wooden buildings serving as a kitchen and a dining hall, surrounded by tents. The meetings were held in the dining hall in the evenings. Margaret was now sixteen years of age, so felt quite grown up when she was allowed to go! The meetings were so enjoyable. Being on holiday she felt totally free to speak, think, pray and read the Word of God. Here was a little bit of heaven on earth. Here was where spirit and soul could soar in song.

It was at this camp that she heard for the first time about the baptism in the Holy Spirit. The speaker said God could come into your heart after conversion and fill your heart to overflowing, Acts 2:4; 19:6. Margaret was as hungry as a dog that had not been fed for a week. This could not be missed. She longed for a closer encounter with the living God. Six young folk, filled with the Holy Spirit, decided to meet with Margaret in a tent, to seek the face of the Lord. They would stay there as long as it took for the Lord to speak to them. Many prayers were saturated with tears. There was much agonizing, wrestling and soul searching as each one prayed. The Holy Spirit seemed to come from nowhere, and Margaret felt a tremendous surge of power from her head to her feet. The power seemed to rest on her tongue as she began to speak in a language that she had never learned, Acts 2:4. Here were new languages given by the Holy Spirit. Each of them were expressing their love to God through another language. As Margaret began to speak in another language, a young woman, Jackie, who was part of a church group gave the interpretation, 1 Corinthians 12:10; 14:13. Margaret discovered that part of what was said in the interpretation of tongues was from Isaiah 44:1–5. God was reminding her that

He knew her before she had been formed in the womb. Margaret was chosen of God. There was the further promise of floods being poured upon the dry ground. Margaret's seed and offspring were to be blessed. This was fulfilled in the days that opened up before her, as first one in her family and then another came to know Jesus Christ as Saviour. Later, at one baptismal service, twenty-seven members of Margaret's family were present when her brother and father were baptised in water.

Bethel church, Royston, Barnsley became the spiritual home of the young convert to Christianity. It was to this church that she committed her future, attending all the meetings she could. She had such a hunger for God, and its depth, length, breath and height could not be measured, only treasured. There was never a thought of missing a meeting, despite waiting at the bus stop in dark winter evenings, and a forty minute bus journey each way, and knowing if the preacher spoke too long, and you missed the last bus, you might have difficulty getting home!

However Margaret's father decided that she must cease attending the church, because he felt the journey was too long, and the lane that she had to walk along to catch the bus was too dark. His argument and theology was 'God is everywhere, and He is in all churches.' 'You must go back to the church where you were christened. It was good enough for your mother and myself, and it must be good enough for you.' Margaret felt like a bear robbed of its cubs. To whom could she turn? To Whom would she turn? She began to pray effectually, and God answered her prayer in a wonderful way, as miraculous to this new convert as any miracle in the New Testament.

Silvanus Warwick, Margaret's father was a religious man, although not born again of the Spirit of the Lord, John 3:7. Religiously, every Sunday morning, he listened to the morning religious broadcast from the BBC (British Broadcasting Corporation). One particular morning, after Margaret had prayed, there was a preacher on the radio, and his text was Matthew 18:6, 'But whoever shall offend one of these little ones which believe in Me, it were better for him that a millstone were hanged about his neck, and that he were drowned in the depth of the sea.' The preacher had a rasping voice, and kept repeating this text. Every time he repeated it Margaret's father trembled more and more, as if he was being blown apart by a strong wind. When he could not take any more of what the man was saying, he looked at Margaret, like a man on a mission, and said, 'Alright, you can go to whatever church you want!' Margaret ran weeping upstairs, and began to thank the Lord for an answer to prayer that resulted in her continuing in her new found love and experience, where joy was unlimited.

One night, Margaret had another dream in which she saw a field filled with golden corn that was 'white unto harvest', John 4:35. She began in the dream to ask God where the reapers were. If nobody would reap the field it would be destroyed. Then, as she looked across the field, it suddenly turned into a loaf of bread, such as she had seen in her mother's kitchen, rising out of the tin as the dough was baked. This was fresh baked bread coming out of the oven in the middle of the field. The loaf of bread broke open, and to her disgust, it was filled with crawling, wriggling worms! She looked away in disgust and anguish, and as she glanced back she saw that a fire had passed over the loaf and the field, and everything had been burnt into a cinder.

She turned her eyes away, then looked again, and the scene changed as if it had been part of a film. There was no corn, no loaf, no cinders, and no evidence of fire but a church full of people who were praying. Many of these people were older people, because she could see grey hair, some of which looked like snow on the mountain top.

In yet another dream, it seemed as if Margaret was attending a meeting when she was inspired by the Holy Spirit to speak in another language. A leader from the group interpreted, 1 Corinthians 14:13, but she herself was not able to hear what was said. It was as if it had to be a secret kept from her. Suddenly, as the man was interpreting, there was the sound of a mighty, rushing wind, and it filled all the church even as it had happened in Acts 2:1–4. The wind seemed to come from the right of the building, and then spread to all parts. The dream ceased as the morning light streamed through the open curtains, as mother came to wake her daughter.

Margaret asked the Oversight of the church what they thought about the dream. They admitted they thought it was from God, but did not know the interpretation. It did seem as if, in a dream, God had revealed to Margaret the history of the church she attended, how He would cleanse the church, then fill it with His Spirit. From this experience the Bread of Life would be offered with no worms, no hypocrisy, and no ulterior motives. It would be a Spirit filled church that would reach out and touch the lost for Jesus Christ. The harvest would be brought in, but in God's time, and using God's methods.

It was shortly after this that Margaret's sister Gwen came to know Jesus Christ as Saviour. The two of them formed a duet, and they would visit many churches to sing, after which Margaret would preach. They were aglow with the glory of the Lord. Many were blessed and touched by their singing, testifying and preaching. It was the Lord's way of training Margaret for her future ministry, firstly in pioneer work, and then in established churches.

Margaret later became a college student, travelling from Wakefield, Yorkshire to Kenley, Surrey, where she met her future husband, Terry Atkinson. He had just returned from Australia, and entered Theological College to prepare for the work of the Lord. Their courtship was swift and sweet, and they were married in August 1964. They then went on to pioneer work, to pioneer a church in Gainsborough, Lincolnshire. They have pioneered and pastored seven churches, covering an area from Lincolnshire to Yorkshire, Lancashire and Cumbria, England. They have travelled abroad many times to minister the Word of God, seeing God confirm His word with signs following, Mark 16:17,20. They have one daughter, Lindsay, two sons, Marcus and Howell, and four grandchildren.

3

PRAYER AND THE PROPHETICAL IN PIONEERING

The work was hard and the people were few as we met together in the local Co-operative hall, the pulpit just a table and a cardboard box. There was no guaranteed stipend, the offering being less in pounds and pence than the number of people in the meeting. What the new converts gave you lived on, and some of them believed that you should live 'on' faith, and not 'by' faith. Sometimes in the offerings there was not enough to keep the proverbial church mouse alive. After paying my national insurance stamp there was only the meagre mite left. You did not have to be an accountant or a mathematician to add the figures up. One line on the receipt book was large enough and long enough to write it all down. There was no suspicion of your hand becoming weary, holding the pen as you added the numbers; no need for you to go beyond counting on your fingers.

A series of children's outreach meetings had been arranged, with a ventriloquist called Francis Lamming, and his young assistant. Hilary, Margaret's sister, joined the team of helpers. The church could not afford accommodation, so Margaret had to take them into her home and provide for them. What she had seemed so small when shared among so many. When she went to the money that was held in the pot, there was only the pot, and whatever had been in it had disappeared. If only she could go to the end of the rainbow and the pot of gold, but instead of going to the end of the rainbow, the decision was made to go to the foot of the Cross. There was no one to turn to except the Lord as Jehovah Jireh.

Margaret went to the 'secret place of the Most High' with the consolation that there was nowhere else to go. With the fullness of conviction in the Lord's 'My God shall supply all your need according to his riches in glory by Christ Jesus,' Philippians 4:19, the prayer warrior came to pray. Armed with a promise, she entered the battlefield, expecting victory. In her heart was the emblem that used to be on genuine Cornish silver: a lamb and a flag: the lamb for shed blood and the flag of victory. Determined, she came out from the place of prayer with more than she had taken in. Would the Lord who has given man the gift of speech grant her a word of prophecy about the need that was present in hungry mouths? There was not enough food in the larder to feed sparrows. She knew if God cares for sparrows He also cares for sorrows. If the God of glory cares for each child as if that child was the only one, He would care for her in the realm of finance and needs met.

Her needs could be measured by the hand of God. Margaret did not go to borrow from God but to give to Him. As she gave, so she received a word from the Lord about the situation, and that would be given at the evening meeting pressed down, shaken together and running over. She left that prayer time with the required money already in her heart, and with a list of things that it could be spent on! Love had become the shopping list. In prayer the cheque had been written out in the words spoken to her by the Lord, all she had to do was to fill in the amount. Not knowing what the costs of keeping these people would be, it was left with the Lord to decide, because when He gives it is as one who is rich beyond measure.

The Lord had revealed to Margaret that a certain man named Arnold Astwood, a businessman who sold fruit, would visit the meeting, and through him God would supply our need. He would give Terry, her husband, a gift that would meet the financial need at this time. There would not be one hungry mouth when the meal had been eaten. After preparing the meal the gift having been received, Margaret saw a number of chickens, eggs and bacon enter the ministry that day, as each one devoured the food set before them, provided by a God with a large storehouse.

There were not many attending the meeting. That night, as Margaret saw the numbers, her heart could have faltered if she had based what the Lord had told her on the people who were present, but this in her heart was not a word from a man but a promise from God. She remained steadfast in faith, even though there seemed to be no physical way that the Lord could answer her prayer. As the meeting progressed, Arnold Astwood came in. He had commenced his business in the London area as a 'barrow boy' selling fruit, but because he had honoured the Lord, the Lord had honoured him with riches, shops and a beautiful family. He used his finance for the work of God, and when he gave a gift with a smile he would say, 'This one is on the Tax Man!'

The meeting came to the end, and as Arnold was leaving, he spoke a few words of encouragement to Terry. As he shook his hand, he passed something into the palm of Terry's hand, and then moved swiftly away. Terry put the envelope into his pocket, and forgot about it until he arrived home. Then Margaret wanted to know if the man she mentioned had given me a gift, and how much had he given? Margaret was not disappointed; the cloth was cut and measured to the need. The gift given would meet every need during the period of time that these workers were staying with us.

The God who owns the cattle on a thousand hills and the wealth in every mine had sold a few cattle, and some miners must have paid their monthly tithe that day!

During the next few weeks Margaret decided to attend a missionary rally in Lincoln. There would be an appeal for support for the missionary, but again Margaret could see the bottom of her purse. She often felt like 'Old Mother Hubbard' who went to a bare cupboard. As the time approached for the meeting, prayer was made, asking Jehovah to supply the need, so that support could be given to the missionaries. Margaret was told by God that the money would arrive, and she would be able to contribute to the needs of the missionary. Margaret knew that the need would be met, but the Lord never told her how it would be met. Would Arnold Astwood come again? Would the Lord use ravens or other means that He had used so many times before? All these questions would only be answered when the need was met.

On the day of the meeting, in the morning post was an envelope that contained a gift which a woman had been prompted to send to Margaret. That postman appeared as an angel to minister to a saint. That gift was to meet the need, to be an evidence of answer to prayer. Although it was a substantial gift, all of it was deposited into the offering for the missionary. Charity begins at home but it does not conclude there. On each note

Margaret saw the picture of the missionary it was given to, and it seemed to her that it all belonged to the one in need. The Scripture came into her heart, 'Freely you have received, freely give,' Matthew 10:8. Margaret had been used as a stopping off place for the gift. It came to her to be passed on to another. The Lord knew He could trust her to bless with the blessing that she had been blessed with. All she had to be was a mirror to reflect what God had given.

An Evangelist had arrived in town, and was staying with Margaret and Terry. Margaret had managed to get enough money together to buy some stew meat, but that was all. Where could she get the carrots, onions, cabbage or peas from? It would not be right to set before the preacher a plain plate of stew. As with spirituality, so with meals, they must be balanced. Margaret went to the God she loved, to seek His face and listen to His voice, then to see His hand at work, as His feet led her to the source of supply. Within the promises of God there was not only meat but additions and one of the additions required was the provision of vegetables. If God could provide one thing He could provide another, and, therefore all things, for He gives again and again, 'pressed down, shaken together and running over.' He gives as nature gives through a harvest, until the barns are filled. His arm would not be shortened when it came to adding to that already provided.

As she prayed, the Lord told her that the plate which she would set before the Evangelist would be full and overflowing. Enough for a king would be served. Appetite would be captivated by what was on the plate.

Seven miles away from that area was a man who had his own allotment, growing many vegetables, as he liked, and this had been an abundant year. While in the allotment and among the vegetables the Lord spoke to him as if he had been in the Garden of Eden. As he was picking his vegetables, his wife came into the garden, and from her sounded the voice of God. God had told her what to say to him. 'Pick some extra, enough for that couple engaged in pioneer work, and make sure you give them plenty, the last time I saw that woman Margaret she looked thin. A sprout or two could do the trick!' This woman gave the bag of vegetables to her son-in- law to deliver them, but he, not having heard from God, delayed bringing them to us. God's delays are not detours, He was waiting for the fruit to ripen under His sun and moon and until the bag was filled, and the taste of heaven went into those vegetables. A table was being prepared in the wilderness.

Margaret had told someone that the Lord was to supply the need, to arrange other things to put with the meat. When the vegetables did not arrive on time, one person said 'I thought you said God had told you that the 'greens' would be sent for the meat.' Margaret thought: Has this person read Psalm 23 "He makes me to lie down in 'green' pastures"? The 'greens' from the green pastures had been promised, and what God promises He provides. There had been enough food for that day, but what about the next day? This was a hand to mouth existence. It was her mouth and God's hand. Would the offering of meat alone satisfy the hungry guest? Maybe Margaret should pray that he would be a vegetarian!

The next morning puffing and blowing as if he had been chasing a train, a young man arrived at the door with a bag full of produce, so full the carrots and beans were peeping over the sides of the bag. He dropped them off his shoulders, and grinned as if two large burdens had been removed. There were so many vegetables, enough to feed many evangelists for many days.

Margaret went on in the power of the prophetical for many days. The young man began to apologise, 'I should have brought these yesterday, but I was delayed.' The delay only strengthened Margaret's faith; those vegetables, so tasty, they tasted like manna from heaven, fresh from the hand of God. God had provided the vegetables, and she must prepare them with as much dedication as the Lord had provided in answering her prayer.

In my opinion women are far more fashion conscious than men. A man will accept most things whether they are in fashion or out of fashion. Some men are colour blind when it comes to fashion. To men, caring about what to wear and whether it matches or not is a fussy thing. As long as it fits and the body is dressed, warm and well fed it will be alright. To be fashionable to some is to wear a raincoat when it is raining. The height of fashion to some men is to wear a tie, and not to have an open necked shirt. To most women, it has to be right. If it is summer then it must be summer wear, and if it is winter then what is worn must be as much a part of the season as the Christmas tree is at Christmas.

Colour co-ordination means a lot to women. It must be all of one colour, or at least the colours must complement each another. This is good because Scriptures tell us that the Lord hates mixtures. Light and darkness cannot mix together. I have often wondered how women would have accepted, and how easy they would have felt wearing Joseph's coat of many colours. The baby Jesus was wrapped in 'swaddling bands' that were the milk cloths, used to wipe away the excess milk from the udders when milking the cows! Later in life He wore a seamless garment, John 19:23.

Margaret had a pink handbag, but this was out of place when the snow was falling. A pink handbag with brown shoes and a brown dress! It was as much out of place to her as snow in summer. Being practical in her prayers, she took everything in a pioneer situation to the Lord. Here was this woman pioneering in prayer. This was not only a church being pioneered but a woman's faith, learning to trust the Lord with the great and the small. God could not be relegated to the church or to the mission field. To Margaret He was the God of the high street and the God of the dark, dingy cellar. It was the Lord who had clothed the first man and woman in the Garden of Eden, Genesis 3:21. The time had not come for Him to deny His responsibilities to those who trusted Him. This Almighty was as strong in one area as in another. He must be trusted on mountain top, and in the lowest dell. Had he not created the rose and the primrose, the dandelion and the lion?

Margaret took this need of a winter handbag to the God of all the seasons. As she prayed, so God spoke to her, and answered her prayer telling her that the need of a winter handbag would be met. To pray was enough, she would not have to go crocodile hunting in deepest Lincolnshire! He that made the hand to carry things would supply the handbag. Also, in the handbag would be some money to spend, because if the Lord gives it will not only be given in good measure, but pressed down and running over, Luke 6:38. God sometimes provides a car and petrol, aeroplane and pilot. When God sends parcels they are full of good things. He never sends paper through the post or boxes of emptiness. When Pandora's Box was empty of all the evil influences, hope was the only thing left. The Lord takes hold of that hope and enriches it with His mercy and love. Some seem to major on the fact the larger the box the smaller the content. The content would be larger than the carrier, the content more than the casing. When God created the sky He made it contain so many stars they could not be counted, and when you get tired of looking up and your neck aches, then look down and start all over again by counting the number of grains of sand on the seashore.

Margaret's mother, Bessie Warwick, had to go to a showroom to buy some presents. There was a great choice in this place, and she would spend some time enjoying looking at the things she did not need! Bessie did not know about the need of her daughter in far away Lincolnshire, but God Who spans the greatest distance between His fingers knew. He would speak to Bessie in this place, but it would be done in such a way that would be supernatural. God does things in an extraordinary way, to make people extraordinary. There would be no flashing lights, or things leaping out of the Scriptures into her spirit.

As she gazed around the huge warehouse, she saw a handbag that would make a good gift for her daughter Hilary, but when Hilary saw it she thought it was the wrong colour, and seemed to be a little bit old fashioned for a younger woman to carry, so she rejected it. It seemed as if the handbag would be thrown away or discarded for something else. It had to be a handbag that mother had to buy, she felt sure of that, but if it was not for Hilary who was it for? Bessie felt that in buying this handbag she was on a mission, this small item was part of a larger plan that would be revealed.

After Hilary rejected the handbag, God spoke to Bessie, 'That handbag was offered to the wrong person. You have bought it for Margaret.' This was a change of tack. Here was a new line of thinking. There and then, under the authority of the Spirit of God, Bessie snatched victory from the jaws of defeat, and what was a gift rejected would become a gift accepted. One woman's poison would become another woman's meat. It would be just the thing to complement her daughter Margaret. Bessie believed that the Lord did not want her to just simply give Margaret the handbag. 'Give it and something more,' were the words that entered into her spirit. 'Put something into it that will make it worth a lot more.' Let there be more on the inside than there is on the outside, as it should be with every believer. The handbag was opened, and as she put money into it Bessie was adding the fragrance of love. That day a gift was added to a gift that would complete the dress of a servant of Jesus Christ. When Margaret saw the handbag it was the one she had been told that she would receive. It was the Lord's way of confirming His word with signs following, Mark 16:20. It was the initial evidence of the fact that the Lord was walking with Margaret as she talked to Him. Here was a handbag that was the right size, the right colour, that matched the dress and the shoes that Margaret already had. Truth even moves into texture if you will allow it. God had turned words of prayer into that handbag. The shape of the handbag was all part of her destiny in Jesus Christ. God is the best; He will dress His children in the best. The King's daughter was all glorious within and without. When He brings them in, He turns them out dressed every day as if it was Easter Day. Every time Margaret used that bag she was reminded to pray to the One who answers prayer. Often, as she put things into the handbag for safe keeping, there was the figure of the Lord filling our lives with good things. Margaret became like a scribe of the kingdom, bringing things out of that handbag old and new, Matthew 13:52. The Lord had put something into it as an answer to prayer in a far off place before Margaret had ever seen it.

4

CRUSHING BURDENS THAT NEED TO BE CRUSHED

Margaret was sitting comfortably in church. The seating was comfortable; the atmosphere was great and glorious. The people were in deep worship, so deep the river of God's Spirit was carrying them along. The Spirit of God began to move on Margaret. Secret things were deposited into her heart for someone, things that were as rare as gold. The problem for Margaret was the person God was speaking to her about was not in the meeting. Margaret went on to automatic pilot, as far as she was concerned she might have been listening to a radio or a voice message. That call of the Spirit was loud and loving, as clear as any church bell on a Sunday morning ringing throughout an English village. It sounded in Margaret's heart as a voice in the valleys and mountains of Wales.

Why was God speaking to her about someone who was absent? Maybe they were in dire need, and could not get to the meeting because of their situation. Margaret sat back, and rested in the arms of the Beloved as much as she rested on the chair. Margaret knew that David 'trusted in the Lord,' suggesting 'rolling himself onto the Lord' as a person would roll themself onto a settee.

We will call the woman Maureen, and the husband Robert. The first word of prophecy that was given to Margaret was for the wife of Robert. God had set the example, for even in revelations from the Spirit it was 'ladies first'. Maureen had been going through a hard time, so difficult it seemed as if she was laying down with her head on a rock. It was so uncomfortable as she turned this way and that, whichever way she turned there was a feeling of trying to sleep with your head on a rock. The pains from the rock were going right through her head as if a nail had been knocked into it. Whichever way Maureen turned, she still faced the rock with her head upon it. This caused her to be unsteady, and there was a lack of sleep, affecting her eyes and her vision. It would make her short tempered. The result was that tiredness took the place of truth. In some areas Maureen felt like the dead among the living, a walking, talking, working zombie. When would the resurrection happen and lift her from this everlasting sleep and daze? What she was experiencing was making everything unreal. She had to try even harder to work for the Lord because of this crushing condition, but in that condition angels would come to break the rock that had been her pillow, and minister unto her where the pain had been. That brought by angels would be from another world, different from the world of pain, frustration and anxiety that Maureen had been encased in. The time of singing and angels flying to and fro had come. Angels would minister into her spirit. It would not be a surface top evolution, but something deep, deeper than hell and as high as heaven. The pain that Maureen had suffered had its source in the difficult time she was passing through, but the ministry of the angels that would come to her in many forms would be unlimited. Where the pain had attacked the brain, the Holy Ghost would bring to her a gift of healing for her condition.

Even in the depths of suffering Maureen still wanted to witness for Jesus Christ. This suffering was identifying her with the cross and with Jesus Christ. At the heart of the pain was the pain of the heart that the Lord would minister to. Out of that pain and suffering a whole new ministry of compassion would come. The bird with the broken wing would fly again. Pain comes and goes, but what the Lord would do for one of His children would come to stay, as Christ Himself applied healing hands.

Her future ministry and testimony would be taken care of. Maureen loved to travel and speak. That witness would be revived, and Maureen would be like a flag at the top of the flag pole signifying that the King was in residence. The colour of the flag was the red, white and blue of redemption. When it seemed as if the witness in the flag would become limp, the wind of God would blow upon it with a fierce Pentecost. All around would be caused to look up as the flag was unfurled in the wind.

What was being given by the Spirit to Margaret tied in with Scripture, because she knew in her heart that in Genesis 22:1, where it says that the Lord did 'tempt' Abraham, that word 'tempt' signifies the unfurling of a flag. The trial that Maureen had passed through was the unfurling of the flag. It would fly where it had never flown before, and would be seen where it could never have been seen before this suffering entered into Maureen's heart. Flags are only raised to the top of the flag pole by effort. The cords of His love would raise the flag as the heart and witness of Maureen for all to see. God's hands were the hands that would raise the flag of destiny.

Maureen was not attending this meeting. She lived a number of miles away, so Margaret decided to write her a letter containing the prophecy she had received. The next day, the postman delivered unto Maureen that also which had been delivered unto Margaret. Maureen opened the letter with curiosity and conviction. Who was writing to her? The pain had told her that the plan of God was in pieces smashed at her feet, everything broken and empty. With trembling fingers that communication was opened. As Maureen began to read what had been written, in her soul the songs of Zion began to be sung by an unseen choir. Each psalm seemed to enter into her spirit as an army of singers and players. Her harp was taken from off the willow tree, Psalm 137:2. She could sing the songs of Zion. The pain seemed to disappear into the paper she was reading. Here was a letter that was better than a prescription from a doctor; it was a prescription from the great Physician, healing her soul. Maureen could hear the stone crumbling, the bits being broken, and as they broke they were appearing as diamonds, glistening in the morning light. It was morning in her heart! It was morning in her heart! It was so good to be alive and kicking instead of being kicked.

After receiving the letter as good news from afar, and soothing her spirit, Maureen decided to reply to thank Margaret for her ministry and faithfulness in passing on what God had given to her, just like the disciples had passed on the miracle bread when five thousand were fed from a few loaves and fishes.

Dear Margaret,
Thank you so much for writing the prophecy down for me. I thank God for showing the revelation to you as you do not know me.

You were such a blessing and encouragement. Now I know that the seven dreadful years are over and my health is coming back. I have gone through such suffering that as a nurse I never understood can happen to anyone.

What you said on the phone was so true, as I was preaching in Finland in October; the anointing from heaven was so great that I had not experienced before. 'Nets full' of people came to Jesus. You are a great witness for His glory!

The next thing Margaret received to pass on was for Maureen's husband, who was in the meeting. Margaret could not give it to him immediately because the meeting was in progress and God was doing other things in this atmosphere.

The same place, the same meeting, but this woman's husband was present. When the appeal was given, he did not venture to the front, but stayed in his seat. After the service Margaret made a 'bee line' to where he was, and began to tell him what the Lord had shown her. Margaret saw Robert was in a tough place, a place as solid and as unyielding as a rock. It was like a rock without any shape, just ragged, broken off from the main mountain, ready to resist what came to it. Robert's life had been as hard as any rock. He had dwelt between a 'rock and a hard place'. Dynamite would not move this structure of rock. Margaret knew that the word for 'power' means 'dynamite', and the Spirit of the Lord was going to split this rock, and shape it until what had been solid and resisting would be able to be used for the glory of God. The rock was too heavy to be lifted or carried away. The only way its influence would be altered was by a miracle from God.

If you go to the area called 'The Pennine Chain' in England you can see how the wind has shaped many rocks, and caused indentations by its constant blowing. There are lovely patterns formed on the rock face by the blowing wind; water with the hard snow has chiselled the rocks into different shapes. Maybe the Lord would do that in Robert's life? His circumstances had become unbearable and unbelievable, and they needed to change. Sometimes the Lord does not change our circumstances, He changes us, then we change the circumstances, If God doesn't change the circumstances, He changes the man to change the circumstances. A man said to his friend, 'How are you today?' The friend replied, 'As well as can be expected, and I expect to be well!' The answer to a prayer is not to get out of bad circumstances or to throw them away, as a stone into a stream, but to use them more than they have used you.

God, the arranger and breaker, was telling Margaret what He intended to do in this man's life. The hardness, the unbearable thing, the darkness, that which seemed to be misshapen and of no use at all, would be taken and used for the glory of

God. Here was another Peter going to be made out of a piece of rock. Suddenly what was a huge rock of suffering and darkness would become like the base of a fountain with many jets of water that would seep through the fissures. Where there was no water for refreshment there would be water that would ooze out of that unpleasant experience. These waters were the tears Robert had shed, but God was turning them, along with his prayers into living, healing and breaking waters. The waters began small, and then covered the rock, until the rock disappeared, as if it was meaningless. In this, one ministry would cease while another would commence. Robert would come to an experience in God, where the difficulties would be forgotten, and in the 'flow' would be the 'know' that came from the knowledge of God. Instead of the hardness of the rock, the tears and water would become part of his ministry. The tears would be turned into healing waters.

As Margaret prayed for Robert, what had been a clouded and worried face with the lines of endurance written across it suddenly became a face of sunshine. All the hardness melted. The rock features had given way to features filled with feeling. Robert began to flow with what the Lord wanted to do. He looked in his spirit for the rock, and all he could see was waters oozing out of the fissures that had appeared in this piece of granite. God was taking and using what had been against him and making it work for him. These waters began to heal all the cuts, bruises and hurts caused by his circumstances. God had proved that He was the Lord of all circumstances. Whatever is wrong can be made right. 'All things' good, bad, evil or pleasant can work together for our good. As the waters flowed so the rock disappeared, never to appear again.

5

DEALING WITH THE SCIENTIFIC MIND

Mark Hall was a student at Salford University. He had attended a Pentecostal meeting, and as it drew to a close, decided to talk with Margaret. There was nothing this young Christian liked better than a cup of good English tea, and conversation. He loved speaking to mature saints; they added something to his life. To him, Margaret was one of those saints who always brought blessing into his life. Her cup always seemed to be full and running over, and through conversation he hoped the secret of that overflowing cup might be revealed. Speaking to Margaret was more than just a conversation, it was fellowship. Many have come to visit and to pray for her, yet as they left have remarked how they went to minister but were themselves ministered unto. There was a constant overflowing of a cup in Margaret's life. As God poured in, she poured out.

As Mark sat at her side, she looked at him, said a few words, then put her hands on him and began to tell him something about his future. It was as if Margaret was reading his autobiography because she said things that made his ears burn and his heart miss a beat. Mark felt like Peter on the Mount of transfiguration. 'Lord, it is good for us to be here.' Margaret had no idea that he was a student where he was studying, or the degree he was aiming for. To Margaret he was just a needy young man requiring help from the Lord. That 'help' would be given in the form of sound words from the heart of the Lord. Margaret would be the springboard the words would come from into the heart of the young man she was praying for.

Things were hard for Mark Hall and he had some difficult decisions to make. He was glad that the decisions of being born and dying were not left to him but to the Lord God Almighty, the Maker of . . . . He knew that in the making of the decision is the making of the man. The carving and curving of the carpenter's tool is part of his decision when to shape a thing of beauty. Mark Hall was in the hands of the Carpenter of Nazareth.

To make a reasoned decision about his future, he required something from the Lord. What the Lord revealed became part of his future. God did not reveal it all, but little by little. He knew his future was woven around the finger of Jesus Christ, set as a golden ring complete with seal in it. Mark was another young man that God told Margaret to speak to. Her heart was filled with the Holy Spirit and the word of the Lord was encased in the Holy Spirit, as a baby in the fluid that surrounds it in the womb.

With strong conviction and the pleading of the Holy Spirit, she began to speak to Mark, words which were for his ears only. Each word was measured with a rod, the rod of God. It was not a word to chide but a word to change, not something that would injure but make whole. Anything that was loose in this young man would be tightened to operation point. That which was ready to fall off would be made secured. As a word promoting growth it would come to fruition. This was no partial plan that God had. There was no plan 'B' only plan 'A'. God doesn't have a different plan matching every letter of the alphabet!

Mark would enter into a laboratory, and take hold of a test tube, and as he took hold of it, he would hold it up to the light. The measurements, quality and quantity must be right. Mark had to commence with the small details and add to them for it all to be scientifically verified in order that his superiors would acknowledge what he was doing. It was more than an experiment; it was part of the Eternal plan for his life. He wanted to make a discovery among the fluid he was handling but it had been elusive in the past, and it was the same at this moment.

Mark was in exploratory science, seeking to make a breakthrough in the area of cancer and other major diseases, but Margaret knew none of these things. To her the young man she was prophesying over was part of the world where God ruled. Whether he was looking to make a breakthrough in medical science or just looking for a needle in a haystack was not important. The important thing was not even the discovery that Mark was about to make. The important thing was that he heard the word of God, and acted upon it. That which was spoken to this man must not be as a stutter, Margaret must not give an 'uncertain sound', because if she did who would prepare him for battle? 1 Corinthians 14:8. The trumpet call and command must be heard as in the stillness of the early morning. She only knew what was being revealed to her by the Spirit of the Lord.

Mark was wearing a white coat like those who are in a pharmacy or doctors in a hospital. He was as busy as a bee in summer. Margaret had only ever seen him dressed in a suit with shirt and tie, now he was wearing suitable attire to make a discovery in the medical world. Mark moved from bench to bench, from test tube to test tube, examining each one carefully, and pouring out its contents into another container to be tested to the point of verification. A number of vapours filled the air. He was standing near a bench filled with round glasses and test tubes with wires and machines around. There were varied but they meant something and were useful. Vapour was coming from some of the tubes, liquid was rising and falling, and there was a hissing sound. Here was a young man with the tools of his trade, and he was using all of them to accomplish what no other had ever accomplished. To him, this was as large an undertaking as climbing Mount Everest or going into 'free fall' from an aeroplane. There was an excitement beyond words. He had the look on his face of a conqueror of the world's highest mountain or a footballer who has just scored the wining goal.

It was in a laboratory like this that the course of history and mankind had been altered. It was in such a laboratory that Dr. James Simpson discovered chloroform, or Dr. Fleming discovered penicillin. Radium and many other such legacies were discovered in these conditions. So many cures had commenced in a laboratory with someone burning the candle at both ends. It was in areas like this that bad bacteria would meet their match, and the death knell would be sounded over their existence.

Then Margaret said a profound thing to him. 'Mark you will make a great discovery, and God is going to give you the answer to the problem that is before you in your research work. That which does not make sense, and is in the infancy stage, will be revealed to you, and the answer will be given to you. You are to discover a potion that will bring health and healing to the world.' Mark looked shocked! Here was a woman who knew nothing about the science of medical healing telling him that he would make a discovery. Either Margaret, not knowing what the young man did, was making it up, or through her God was speaking into his soul. How did she know that he was working on a certain project, trying to find the answer that so far had eluded him?

Suddenly, test tubes and laboratories did not mean a thing, but this word from God meant everything. Here was God saying that He would confirm His word with a sign, a sure sign of success. Here was a promise from the Lord that would be fulfilled in Mark's workplace. If that word did not touch those around him, and others, it was not worth receiving or repeating. Mark would live in what was said for many days, months and years. The unexpected, the unexplained would be expected and explained. It would become part of him, and be put into practise when the promise was fulfilled.

There were those who would gladly recognise God in a church, in a home or on the street, but not in a laboratory. This is where the evolutionist plies his trade. It seemed as if the door to such a place was closed by an atheist. God could be everywhere except in a hospital in the research department, yet God was telling Mark that He would be right where he was in his laboratory. Mark would be dressed in his white coat, God would be dressed in invisibility, but the proof of where He was and what He was would be in the discovery. God would come through a test tube with an answer to the prayers of this young Christian!

Mark left that church hall full of praise for a magnificent God, and believing what had been said to him would happen. That night there were no clouds in the sky, it was filled with bright shining stars, and the moon seemed like a half circle of yellow gold. Mark could have not been happier if his left foot had been hallelujah and his right foot amen as he walked along the street into his home. Mark looked forward to his studies, there was a gleam in his eye, lightness in his step, and relish in his heart, because he believed the word of God, that he would make a discovery, and that discovery would help others.

To be the first in anything is a marvellous achievement, but to be the first because God has said so is even greater. The Almighty receives the honour, praise and glory. Even in his work Mark would not stop glorifying God in word, deed and praise. Many silent prayers would be offered in the days to come to a God Who can hear in the silence of a prayer. Quietness is the essence of what God is.

Mark had a heart for people. His was an evangelical nature, and whether by testifying or discovering he wanted to glorify the Creator of all. What had been a puzzle to him and many others was to be resolved, because he believed and received what had been said to him through Margaret, an empty vessel with no idea of the work he was involved in. Mark went to work the next day in the ascendancy. He was walking in resurrection life and on resurrection ground.

Some time later, Mark telephoned Margaret to tell her how God had fulfilled His word, and what had happened to him since he received that prophecy. Margaret asked him to write a letter, and to send it to her. Here is what Mark Hall wrote to Margaret, a jubilant letter of praise and thanks to the Lord of all glory.

'I am on a degree course called Biochemical Sciences at Salford University, and I am currently on a placement. This means instead of going into my final year of studies, I went on a placement where you gain more practical experience. My placement for the past year has been at Christies Hospital, Manchester in the research laboratories at 'Peterson Institute for Cancer Research'. (PICR) PICR works very close with the hospital and my department in the PICR is Drug Development, where new drugs are discovered, tried and tested. Only five places were available in the whole institute for students in the UK. God gave me this position and He favoured my

application, because He wanted to fulfil His will in my life. I thank God for this position, and I know He is guiding me into the right paths. Paths of discovery and destiny.

'My work in PICR was to come up with a simple method of detecting an enzyme in the patient. If the enzyme is present in the patient (96% of the population of the UK have this enzyme!) then the patients are eligible for new drugs, which can destroy cancer! This can be done with a pinprick of blood from the thumb, and then by looking at the genes. I have set this method up, which means we have a kit set up and running that was designed by me! We can easily get samples and give patients a new drug within the next four months.

'Margaret met with me, and later I telephoned her to tell her of the fulfilment of a prophecy she had received from the Lord about my future work in medical science. Margaret had no idea where I worked, the nature of my work, or what I was praying about and trying to do. Margaret thought I was still at college, but God revealed to her things about me that would affect my future. My consolation revealed that my future is in the Lord.

'Margaret had seen me working in a laboratory, wearing a white smock (a lab coat which I always wear at work) and I was mixing solutions (chemicals). God had revealed to her that I was going to discover a potential mixture that would heal people.

'*A week after Margaret had contacted me, one Chinese doctor who works at Manchester Medical School and who came to PICR to use the equipment, was speaking to me. He said that he could see I was very enthusiastic in my work and that my results were so good, they should be published. He also said that I could go to his labs after University and do a PhD with him. Wow! It took my breath away to receive an offer from such an eminent man of medical skill and healing. Not wanting to do anything suddenly or anything that would jeopardise my future I asked my supervisor Ted about the man. Ted told me he was trying to use me for my results and things that I had discovered. I was disappointed to hear this but I obeyed my supervisor and turned down the offer from the Chinese doctor.*

'*A couple of months later I was approached by my supervisor Ted, and he asked if I would work on an experiment that other students had tried but failed. This would be a challenge of the first magnitude! He told me that my University tutor and I would produce a paper, and that I had the ability to get good results even where others had failed. He would publish a paper with me on what I was being asked to do. God is so good to us! He gives us the desire of our heart so that we can give the glory back to Him. It is very unusual for a student who had still not obtained a degree to publish a paper. God was going to use me to fulfil what He had promised, and to show others what He could do. Then I could tell them what He had done!*

'At present I am busy finishing the experiment and writing my Project about the placement year. I am going to put on my Acknowledgement Section a thank you to God, so that people can read and understand where my knowledge came from.

'Christians in Christies Hospital meet together on Tuesdays for prayer. We have a notice board, and others are invited to pin prayer requests on it. We take these requests and ask God for healing and help. Sometimes I get to see patients who tell me they have been healed after we have prayed for them. They write a note of thanks and pin it on the notice board. One patient who was called the 'badge man' was told by doctors that he had the big 'C' (cancer), he said, 'Yeah, I know I have Jesus Christ in my life.' He was cured after treatment, and his cancer did not return. Many Christians work in PICR, and this is a great witness among the hard scientists in the Institute.

'I now work testing new drugs. The vision passed on to me by Margaret was a sure confirmation of the work that the Holy Spirit is doing in Christie's Hospital. I am here as a shining light to those in darkness. Thank God for the prophetical and the personal touch.'

6

THE FRUIT OF THE SPIRIT

Margaret Atkinson was never strong physically but in spiritual character she was a giant among men. She was an introvert, of a quiet disposition but with an inward strength that would match a range of mountains. There was a sense of strength in her life that was seen rather than heard. Margaret was no boisterous woman; she never raised her voice to command a situation. All things were brought into captivity by a meek and quiet spirit. When nothing worked she believed that prayer would, and the evidences of that was in those things given her to pass on to others from the Lord.

There was a determination born within her that was taken and used by the Spirit of God. The spider's thin thread of gossamer may not be very strong, but when woven together can produce something strong and so virile. Once God had revealed something to Margaret, the conviction was so deep that pearl divers and dredgers would not get it out of her. There were times when she had to wait weeks, months and years to see prophecies fulfilled, but in the waiting was the developing of her character. There was conviction that those who 'wait' on the Lord would 'renew' their strength. On many occasions she went into the presence of God as a mouse begging cheese and came out like a lion with honey in its carcase, Judges 14:8,9.

The promises of the Lord to her were more sure and real than the path she walked from her door to the pavement. Margaret was never physically strong, suffering ulcers as a child left her with a weak stomach. That did not become an impediment, but provided a reason to trust the Lord even more. Some of Jacob's greatest acts and revelations were received when he walked with a limp! Although Margaret had a slight lisp she never made this an excuse not to speak for Jesus. There would be no going into heaven on the back of a lame excuse. What she lacked in physical strength she gained in spiritual power.

Long before Margaret prayed for people on a personal level she spent time in deep intercession. In the night time, whether it was midnight or the early hours of the morning, a small light could be seen coming from her bedroom. This was the hour of power, the place of grace, the harbour to which the ship retreated during a time of storm. Margaret would be found interceding for those she loved at any time and in every place. It was at times like this that the Lord revealed many things to her that would become rarer than jewels, more colourful than rubies. Walking by her bedroom door, you would hear a quiet voice pleading with the Lord for one thing and another, then a hesitation followed by a sob, and then the Scriptures would be quoted in her prayers. This was the side of her that even close friends never saw, but they experienced the results of her deep intercession.

For ten years she was the prayer co-ordinator of the church's 'prayer chain' in a local large congregation. At all times of the day when the telephone rang, Margaret would be called upon to pass on the need, and arrange for others to pray in groups that the Lord would meet the need. The answers to prayer recorded were more than the links in the prayer chain! It did not suit Margaret just to receive a prayer request, but many times she prayed for the one making the request and the one in need. She believed in striking while the iron was hot. Her prayers were used as an umbrella, and all were invited to stand underneath it.

In her spirituality, Margaret never neglected her family or housework. Her spirituality was of a practical nature as real as the dress she wore. All she required to do was fruit that was born from the Spirit of God. There were promptings and convictions that could have only come from the Almighty granting her assurances that what she prayed for would be given. She never prayed as a child coming to a reluctant father. To see a prayer answered was to witness the ability of God ministering grace in unmeasured supply. There was nothing cloister about her, or far removed. Margaret operated where the leather from the shoe touched the floor. Whether she was in the local supermarket, in her bedroom in a church, on the street or flying through the air, she would pray. Prayer, to her, was as natural as breathing, speaking or looking. Margaret prayed before something happened, when it happened and after it had happened, so she was rarely caught out by surprise.

It was after much prayer that Margaret met with Valerie Jones. Valerie was a pretty girl with hair as black as soot. She was married to Albert. Coming from South Africa to the north of England there were many things about the English culture that Valerie did not understand, but the common language even in a foreign culture is that of prayer. All pray, all seek God; all receive and see answers to prayer. There were spiritual lessons that she was still learning. There was a deep need in Valerie's life, deeper than any sea, You could identify with how she felt by the look of sadness on her face. The burdens of life were crushing her, causing the instrument of her joy to be out of tune.

Valerie had tried working in a local Christian

bookshop, only to find that her employer was not as Christian as she thought he would be, and she had terminated her employment. At the same time her husband Albert had been made redundant. Here were two of God's children both without an occupation. The occupation of prayer still existed, and they would use that as a springboard into secular employment. They loved the Lord along with their small, growing family. If her husband obtained a position elsewhere in the country then they would have to sell their house, and it was a bad time in England at this moment to sell a house. All these things weighed upon her, crushing her spirit and making it smaller than God intended. What was created to be large became small and restrictive. That meant to be tall and strong was becoming weak and small. Valerie began to pray that God would help them in their situation.

As she prayed, the gracious God took hold of that prayer, and interpreted it with the answer into the spirit of Margaret, who lived just a few yards away. What Valerie sent up in prayer was translated by God to her advantage. Her husband required employment, and they needed to sell the house, and she could do with part-time employment. If only all things worked together for good, for them that loved God! Romans 8:28. At the moment it appeared as if everything was in bits and pieces, and it was lying scattered at her feet. Each small piece contained one of her dreams.

Margaret laid her hands on the shoulders of Valerie and began to unfold her future like the bud unfolding and producing the leaf to adorn the tree. God had heard Valerie's prayer and was going to do something about the things she had requested. He would do that which befitted a King's daughter. It seemed to Valerie as if Margaret was reading from a book, the book of her life and future. How could she know such things and be so assured that what she was saying would happen in Valerie's life? Margaret began by describing her innermost feelings. The burdens, the grey days, the hours of pain and wrestling with her own thoughts were all being revealed.

Margaret began to tell Valerie that the days of poverty were coming to an end. God was going to tie prosperity to the end of her prayer. In the future, Valerie's intercession would not come from a mat of straw but one of silver as she knelt to pray. She had been in a place as a tree without fruit, but the spring and summer of God would change all that. Seeds would be sown into the barren land, and the harvest would appear. The fullness of blessing would accompany the fullness of prayer. The time of the withered fruit was to disappear; the Lord would bring Valerie and her family into a place of fruitfulness. Beulah — a delightsome land — would be before her. The dry bread of the wilderness years would cease, and the corn of the land would be eaten in the next few months. Her husband would find a position, but it would mean him leaving the place where they now lived. God was not going to plant a new tree full of fruit where they were, He was going to take them to a place already planted, an area of fruitfulness. They were to move to the land of fruit trees, where there are apples, and the farm of His fruitfulness.

Margaret told Valerie that she and her family would go to the place of apples and orchards. Wherever she looked, fruit would be hanging from the branches as a token of the favour of the Lord. In fact they would move to the area of cider apples. This would result in the burden being lifted, and she would feel as a fruit tree in autumn. God would take Valerie into something sweet smelling, containing many blossoms and apples, a great orchard. The family who had to share one apple would have many apples to share with others.

Some months later, Albert found his new job. He had to go to many interviews, but during the interviews he had the conviction that the Lord was in charge. Men might say 'yes' or 'no', but when God has said 'yes' and 'yes' in Christ Jesus, then the last word spoken on his application would be 'yes'. It was a word from the Lord which could not fail. As Albert was prayed for, even the clock at the place he was to work in was described. The time and the opportunity were being set before Valerie and Albert. Even leaving his other job was foretold by another prophet who had ministered to Albert. Everything was fitting together like the pieces of a puzzle, that are only a puzzle. They had been brought together as a plan for their future. The hand of God was in their life, and their future was written on His hands. God was in control, moving and directing as the winds blow over blossom and it is turned into fruit. This hand would plant trees, and they would be in an area of orchards growing, not only in their hearts as a sign of fruitfulness but in a practical way as the Lord supplied their need. It would not be supplied in one apple, but in many. One apple with many pips means many apple trees. This is how God was going to answer their prayers.

Blessed is that person who hears they are going to move and begins to pack away unused things, even before they have received the direction they must take. That took a step of faith, to pack before they knew where they were going. Each item packed was an expression of their faith in what the Lord had said.

They were now moving from where they were living to the place of cider apples. Where they lived was a beautiful area of Manchester, but there were certainly no orchards in this place! The new occupation was in Yeovil, the heart of cider making in England. Here was the promise fulfilled of the place of much fruit, many apples and trees. Valerie and Albert would be in the county that was full of them, and many obtained their living through cider apples. Once again, God had triumphed through Margaret who was prepared to give what the Lord had told her to give, and Valerie who was prepared to accept what the Lord had said. Today, the house is sold, the family has increased, and they are enjoying the 'fruit of the Spirit' as provided for them before they saw or tasted one apple. 'O, taste and see that the Lord is good, blessed is the man that trusts in Him,' Psalm 34:8. They were going to experience something sweeter and more stimulating than cider!

What was seed in pip and apple core was turned into fullness by the word of the Lord. God cared enough to speak to help a family in a time of crisis through timeless truth. They had been in an area and had experienced failure and rejection. In God, they would go to the place where apples were crushed, but they as a family would be rosy red and always have the hand of God upon them keeping them fresh enough to admire, and good enough to eat. Apples red and mature awaited them, and they were rejoicing more than the time of the harvest fruit ingathering. They entered into a time of harvest, rejoicing and singing.

7

WRESTLING WITH ANXIETY

I glanced at the clock on the wall, it was 2 a. m. A shaft of light was penetrating the door space between the bottom of the door and the carpet, and meant only one thing, Margaret was reading her Bible. I took a peep inside, and there she was with the Bible spread out over her legs as if it had been a table, and she a sparrow feeding from that table. Margaret loved the Word of God, and her happiest moments were when she was poring over its pages. It seemed as if something from that Word entered her spirit, and like David in Psalm 55:6 she soared in her spirit like a dove. It was her chief joy of the night, there was no longing for the moon, stars or the rays of dawn to enter the room and interrupt the revelation she was receiving from the Lord. This was a time of feasting after fasting, a time to revel in the righteousness of the Lord, as much as the Prodigal son did on his return into the father's fold.

It was at times like this that the Spirit of God began to move upon her, and it was here that fresh revelation, as fresh as the dew on the lawn outside her window, or as manna falling from the skies, came to her and became part of her portfolio.

It was during this season of meditation that God began to reveal the needs of others to her. Sometimes, long before she met the person, that which had been received was kept locked up in her heart as treasure, for nothing would be revealed to anyone other than the person it was intended for. Margaret used to ponder all these things in her heart, Luke 2:19. 'Ponder' meaning turning over and over until settling in their designated position.

God granted her new things to add to the old, not that the old was dry or hard. If ointment was received in a word from the Lord, that ointment would be applied when the wound was made visible. If it was a sharp arrow, then it would not be fired until God revealed the target. If God reveals the target, be it ever so far away it will not be missed. God's words are always sure, and sometimes they completed the chain that had a link missing. What the Lord reveals is that which is needed at a particular moment. When there is part of the puzzle missing, God provides that missing part. If half of what is required is absent, then the Lord supplies the other half, which is the better half, in fact better than the other half, for it acts as the whole. Without the knowledge of God we are blind, dull, unlearned and cannot see afar.

Margaret was never as bold as brass. There was always that which was timorous within her. The nature within was more of the mouse nature than the lion. Stout-hearted but not lion-hearted describes her disposition. The inner life part of the inner sanctum could be described as a mouse that thought it had lion qualities given from the Lion of the Tribe of Judah.

There was a reluctance in her to be seen and heard. There was no bragging or brawling disposition in her. That loud and coarse was as foreign to her as man is from Mars. Can you imagine the impact when the Lord gave her something to do and say, and she had to confront the person that she knew with a favourable message or a message that would convict them? Yet there was never any reluctance to obey the Lord. It would be as a sheep to the slaughter that she sometimes went forth. Fear was defeated by faith, fear was defeated by fact. After the event she could and would always smile at herself, wondering how things would turn out, because, when they did emerge, the work of the Lord in the situation would be clear to see.

Any voice of trembling was overcome as she moved in the echo of His voice. What God said was the important thing, not how Margaret felt. It was sure and real in every aspect. The outcome was not dependent on her emotions but was the product of her devotions. Until she gave to another what had been given by God, it burned night and day as a pillar of fire. There was a persuasive passion within her which drove her on to do what a woman has to do. It could be said of Margaret, as it is recorded of one who was mentioned in the New Testament: 'she did what she could,' Mark 14:8. Only when that which had been received by her was uttered did she feel that the mission had been complete.

Sometimes the revelation was so deep that she found it difficult to put into words. When she met with the one in need, the words would flow through her, not as a quiet stream but as a stream that an elephant could bathe in or a lamb could swim in, as if Niagara Falls flowed into calmer waters as they expanded. That flowed through her lips as if each word was in a race to get there first. She spoke under inspiration.

It was after such a time spent meditating and praying that Margaret sat at the side of Tina. The moment Tina entered the room, Margaret knew that here was a woman in great distress of soul. Here was one that Satan had bound. She was struggling to get free, but the more she struggled the tighter the grip on her life seemed to be. Tina had a hard life. Her husband had been committed to prison. Life had been thorns and thistles for this woman. Left alone to look after her two sons, she was desolate and depressed. Then someone invited her to church, where she heard words that sounded like sweet music to her soul. Tina accepted Christ as her Saviour. A relationship developed between her and the Lord. Tina was in love again! Every bird seemed to have a song, every flower appeared as a personal gift to her from the Lord, telling her that He loved her so much.

Every cloud had a silver lining. Life had suddenly gone from a 'chance' through a change to 'dance'. But Tina felt that there were not enough dance movements or dances written to fully express how she felt at this time. Everything on earth seemed in tune and in time, even on time. Tina asked herself why she had gone through so many years without discovering this way of gladness. Those unhappy years, those hours of sadness, were now far removed, as far removed as the east is from the west.

Margaret was taken by surprise when she sat next to her. The smile of radiance had gone. The face was lowered, the hands tightly clasped together, as if Tina was trying to stop what was left of her experience with the Lord escaping. Here was a woman who had faced the world with a smile and a cheer, now her shoulders were bent as one who was ashamed of something.

There was a battle raging in Tina's heart, and Margaret knew about the battle. What had been straight and true was now twisted and warped. The

Lord had revealed it to Margaret, and she drew alongside Tina as a physician drawing alongside a patient, not to write a prescription, but to administer medicine. There was a deep need here, yet it was not beyond the reach or the depth of the love of God in Christ Jesus.

Tina did not look like an all-in wrester, but a wrestler that was all in! Thin and frail looking, as if she had been on a long journey, she stood before Margaret, cheeks red with heat and worry. The sting of sin was certainly trying to mark her in body and soul. Her eyes were pleading, begging, and looking for answers to her many problems. Tina did not have to speak, for the Spirit of the Lord was speaking to Margaret even before she prayed for her. The heart of this woman had been revealed and the remedy prepared, even before she entered the room and drew alongside the servant of the Lord. Only the Lord can reveal the real, and take care of care as if it never existed. He was about to do a new and a real thing.

'Tina, you have been in a wrestling match! The struggle has weakened your faith, and you have come to the point of perplexity, and this is leading you to want to stop and die. You feel as if you have been left bleeding and dying with no one to help. The trouble and distress of Jacob has entered into your life. At the moment you are in the corner between bouts of fear and failure, and you do not want to come back out because if you do there is the fear that another beating will be yours. The spirit of the loser has latched on to your heart. You feel that you could sooner die than win. Here in this small dark corner, everything is so easy. The person at your side is cooling you with a towel, and is plying you with water. They are applying different lotions to your hands and face with the hope that you can be a winner. Those around you, seeking to help you, feel that you can never win, but it is a shame to give in, so they keep pushing you back into the fight, but you keep coming back to the corner to retire. You have had enough of life, it has become unbearable, and you are vulnerable and breakable. The strain is too great, and it has gone against the grain. Tina, you have requested that they should 'throw the towel in'. You want to give up. There is a lack of will and intensity; that intensity used to be there, for you were a born fighter, but the fire has gone out of your fight, and the light had gone out of your love, and it is fast becoming midnight.'

Then Tina went from her own corner into that which was referred to as 'neutral', and in that corner Tina was aware of the presence and power of God, larger than life and stronger than rock. He began to wipe away the beads of sweat, counting each bead as a pearl of great worth. The marks of suffering on Tina's face were being healed by the grace of God. All the effort of this soul had been noticed by the Lord. God was wiping her brow and giving her a drink. All Tina's strength was as a forgotten memory as she sat in that corner. Here was the position of submission, but when she saw the Lord she stood out of reverence for Almighty God. God said to her, 'Do not throw the towel in, Tina.' That wipe from the cloth that God was holding not only wiped her brow but wiped away the tears of remorse, the sadness, all the frustration, the lean years, the desperation and the darkness of the past few months. One sweep of the Lord's hand, and hell itself was torn from this woman's brow. It wiped off the sadness, and seemed to wipe on gladness which even the word abundance could not aptly describe. As the negative was removed, the positive was put in its place. Tears were being replaced by laughter; misery was becoming the servant of joy.

That which had been ready to give in was being given a drink of water of life. It was so refreshing that Tina's spirit was revived as a fish being put back into water after being hooked and left on the river bank to die. The touch of the cloth of Christ (the face cloth that they covered Him within the tomb), Mark 14:51, 52. was enough to meet every need. God was performing another creation that to Tina was as important as that performed in the Book of Genesis. Unlike those who would have pushed Tina back into the fray the Lord was saying, ' . . . I will go with you into the fight with My might.' If Tina fell she would fall, but if she stood then He would stand with her. There would be no experience that would not be sacred or sanctified by His presence. The warm glow of His love entered into Tina's heart as a balm of comfort and joy.

These words were courage and power to the weakened woman. If He could walk through it all she would walk with Him. It was not now a bell sounding for the commencement of the next round, but a voice, the voice of the Lord, coming to where this woman in need was. Here in the midst of the gore and guts was a voice talking about love. Tina had not realised that the Almighty conquers through love and not hate, not by resisting but by yielding. As she yielded to Him, then all would be well. There would be no death, or falling as you take up the position of worship, you cannot be thrown down, because you are on your knees already.

Tina began to weep; droplets of water began to course down her face and mingle with the sweat. It was as if her tears were glad to get away from her eyes, as if eyes and tears were sworn enemies. Sweet relief covered her face, as if the sun had risen again after a dark, black night. The age of angels and the dispensation of the dynamic were returning to a wayward daughter. There was a new impetus in her life, dynamic was replacing decay.

From that corner God pushed Tina back into

the fight, but not before He had wiped away the sorrow, and blessed that human form with a future and something worth fighting for. This was the fight of life, and she was fighting 'for' and 'with' the Lord, for He had revealed that He was standing by her side. He was out there where the fight was at its strongest and longest. Tina now felt that she had a cause worth living, dying and fighting for.

It was a new woman that left the arms and heart of God, to go into the centre of the ring, to the 'brunt' (the hottest part) of the battle. Well clad, fed, refreshed, and capable, she looked for the opposition with relish. 'Watch out world' seemed to be written all over her face. Here was a runner ready to run a good race at God's pace with God's grace. She wanted enough grace to win and finish.

Margaret's husband Terry had been ministering to people quite a distance from where Margaret and Tina stood, and had never heard a word that Margaret had said. Suddenly, he came over to Tina, after Margaret had finished praying for her, and said, 'Tina, do not throw the towel in! It is not time to give in but to go on! God is with you, mighty woman of valour.'

God had confirmed with a double confirmation that He was in control, and that He wanted this sorry soul to sing again and reflect the glory of God. It was as if the Lord was even going to speak to her a second and a third time, as long as Tina came out fighting in the battle of life.

God in His mercy had turned a loser into a winner. The towel would be retained, turned into a crown that would be worn on the head of the champion. The watching crowd would make way for a champion. The loser would stay in his own corner; the winner goes on from strength to strength. The glory of anything is to see it through to the end, an end that is the beginning of new things in the Lord. With God there is no ending, only a beginning. Learn to smite the fright, learn to smite through Him who set His face as a flint rock.

8

DEMONIC INFLUENCE

It can sometimes be difficult to distinguish between demonic activity and what the Lord wants to do. One has the nature of light, while the other is compared with darkness. Even Satan can appear as an angel of light, 2 Corinthians 11:14 but when rebuked by God that light fades into darkness because the spark has been removed. Satan recedes to his own domain. The gift of discernment is given so that the eyes of our understanding might be clearly opened by the Spirit of God, 1 Corinthians 12:10. There are inner eyes that can see through the ability of the Holy Spirit, Ephesians 1:18.

As Margaret sought the Lord with strong crying, God would sometimes reveal demonic activity in the lives of those she would meet. Long before she saw the person, she saw and recognised the plot, and knew that this activity was part of a scheme of the devil. God plans while the devil schemes, Ephesians 6:12. Stratagem — a piece of generalship. The 'plot' devised by Satan is always undone by a plan that is enacted by the Spirit of the Lord. One is a scheme, while the other is a summary of eternal life. Whenever you get confusion that leads into anarchy the 'master of nothing' has been at work. While praying, Margaret could see what the devil was doing as he sought to plunder God's success with defeat and failure. God meant it for good (weaves it together as a weaver weaves his cloth), while the adversary means it for evil — not woven but just thrown together. There is always the slime mark of the snake wherever it has been. 'Mark the paths of Satan well, and stay away from such devious ways or you will go around in circles,' Margaret thought, as she saw a woman who was being tormented by Satan.

Satan appeared as a demon, and was faceless. There could be no display of fear in its face, but its body could quiver at the mention of the name of Jesus Christ. It had the smallness of an ant, dressed in black, but was desperate about its mission. The hell it was already enduring was that of being unfed, and the fact that it could never grow into anything but a demon unless it could possess a human body. The black shape could never take on any other shape without the help of a human. It was as an ambassador in bonds, dressed in black, a dark night without the moon shining.

Being shapeless it wanted to obtain a form by seeking to influence a woman. It had no personality of its own, and was seeking one that it could express its nature through. It flitted across the field of the human heart as a cloud would scurry before the wind. As it took each step the demon gave furtive glances over its shoulders, then looking all around, yet at the same time was careful where it was treading as if it had entered a minefield as it chased after this believer. It was 'cagey' before it was put under lock and key. It had so much to hide. As it moved along it had the awareness of a Merekat, which stations one of their kind to be a lookout. It knew if it was seen or heard it would be rebuked, and that rebuke would carry it into hell.

There was no place for sunshine or happiness in that dwarf form of a being, dressed in black and looked undernourished. Which was so unlike the caricatures that we see of Satan or a demon. There was no pointed tail, no forked spear in its hand and no crown on its head, no supercilious grin on its evil face. There was the thinness of hunger in its body. This doomed, vile creature lacked expression, and might have been just a stone, unloved, unmoved, and unyielding. It seemed as if it had been tormented, and that torment must be passed on to another. Its ministry was its ability to torment people. It was on a mission without mercy, a mission of cruelty to crush was its objective. It scurried along as if it had been a monkey, using its hands and feet to propel it forward. It never seemed to be still, as if an inner voice was compelling it to go along with speed, as if the time was short and the need was great.

The demon believed in sharing its ministry. This operative of Satan was undernourished, but was planting seeds in the hope of a harvest. Its main meal was to dominate another's spirit in the way in which it was dominated by the devil. You could not see its ribs because they were encased in black shadow. It would reap and feed on what it planted. The seeds were the same shape and size, but the heart of each was different. One was sedition, another seduction, then discord, anger, jealousy, malice and pride. Put these together and you have the menu for a demon. As we look on a menu for food to order and eat, so demons relish human lives that they can exploit. They are hunger driven to tempt others into failure. It was a lip licking, finger licking prospect for this worker with the promise of a banquet in each seed. Demons influence with relish, with far more zeal than some Christians exhibit when doing the work of God. Tares must be sown in the night, tares that look as standing wheat without a closer inspection, Matthew 13:24–40.

The Christian is often surprised to see Satan acting in disguise and disgust as he seeks to imitate all that is Christ and Christian. There in a large field was Satan sowing seed, as if he belonged there and had every right to be sowing in another's field. Here was a disciple in a demon! He could have been mistaken for a Christian worker, if the Lord had not given His servant a spiritual insight into the activity of Satan in Jean's mind and heart. Satan was sowing as methodically and carefully as anyone who has read Matthew 13 about the sower and the seed. This arch enemy had a plan, and that plan was to sow discord among the brethren, and the lady being prayed for was the area that the evil one was seeking to demonstrate his power through. The work of the demon was being passed to the conscripted character of a woman with a different charter than that given by Jesus Christ. Jesus had said, 'Go ye into all the world and preach the gospel,' Mark 16:15. Here from the demon it was 'Go you into all the world and preach the gossip.'

The fires of hell never burn brightly, but they do burn for ever and ever, Revelation 14:11; 20:10. Those flames of torment in temptation that enter into a soul burn a dull yellow, the colour of desertion, rebellion and self will, and the colour that is sometimes used to paint Judas. They burn deeply and surely, converting all before them into a flame from hell that strikes a soul with deep hot passion, anger, rage and jealousy. There is a torment in Satan that can never bear fruit unto eternal life. Whatever he sows are seeds of destruction, seeds of hopelessness, and tragedy. Those seeds sown in evil thoughts and suggestions would be so cutting they would reap their own harvest.

The meeting was coming to a climax; Margaret was peering over the congregation, and saw Jean sitting comfortably. This disturbed Margaret; because she thought as the appeal was given Jean would run out to the front to get help. The woman seemed complacent, as if she did not understand or recognise the need in her heart. It was as if she was set in concrete or a marble statue of a saint. There was no movement of mouth, tongue or eyes, just a blank stare. There she sat, as cold as a statue at the midnight hour. It seemed as if she was waiting for life to catch up with her — or should I say life was waiting for Jean to catch up with it?

Margaret went to Jean and explained what Satan was doing in her life. When she heard Margaret speak, it was as if an axe had been flung at the trunk of a tree with the force of giant hands. Jean began to tremble in tears as one who had been apprehended. A guilty look came on her face, and she turned towards Margaret, waiting, listening for the words of the judge to tell her what her sentence in prison would be.

When Jean had been converted, high hopes had been put into her heart, all that had been torn and destroyed was restored in Christ Jesus. Hopes that the strongest wind would never blow out, and the fiercest flames would never burn out, had been put into her heart. Her life had been one of joy abounding. Her expectancy knew no bounds. Being set free she would seek to set others free. Jean had always longed that her husband and son would commit themselves to the Christ of God, and prayed and worked to this end.

Jean's heart became empty. Jesus said: When a strong man armed keepeth his palace, his goods are in peace: But when a stronger than he shall come upon him, and overcome him, he taketh from him all his armour wherein he trusted, and divideth his spoils. He that is not with me is against me: and he that gathereth not with me scattereth. When the unclean spirit is gone out of a man, he walketh through dry places, seeking rest; and finding none, he saith, I will return unto my house whence I came out. And when he cometh, he findeth it swept and garnished. Then goeth he, and taketh to him seven other spirits more wicked than himself; and they enter in, and dwell there: and the last state of that man is worse than the first, Luke 11:21 – 26.

If a person is set free and they do not find fulfilment to fill up their life, then they take unto themselves that which will ultimately destroy them. Jean had been like a house with the furniture in order, and the door knocker sparkling as if it had been polished. Then she began to get bored with the order of things, and sought excitement in those things which are unexciting yet so inviting.

As time went by the scenery not only changed but the sincerity of Jean was altered from that which had been good and wholesome into something resembling hypocrisy. Jean entered into a period of loneliness and despair. Instead of trusting in the Lord she trusted her own emotions. She had a 'roller coaster' experience, going up and down, sideways and lurching forwards. If she felt down then down she went. If she felt as high as a kite into the heavenlies she would go. Sometimes she soared, at other times she sank. There were moments when in faith and experience Jean went into free-fall, not knowing where or how she would land. Living on her emotions she became emotional.

Jean would have a good cry as she gave her version of events, rather like a fish looking through water to the surface of the river as she passed on old news, new news but not good news. Whenever somebody said no, and she wanted them to say yes, she took a steep nose dive into that where there seemed to be no return. She wanted to rule others by her emotions instead of working with them as the Spirit of God led her. To rule your emotions you must learn to follow Jesus and walk on water. You are either floating in the boat or walking — the choice is yours. Will you trust the boat that can be smashed by waves, or trust the Rock that breaks the waves? Do not try to walk on water if you can't stand on the Rock!

Apart from all this, Jean became the devil's map of interference and activity. Her mind and heart was being taken over as a dark shadow entered into it. Here was a willing disciple of the devil, so different from a disciple of Jesus Christ. The imitation was easy, but the limitations were great. God loves us more and more, while the devil sees to it that more and more murder and hate is sown into the soul, commencing with Cain who killed his brother, in the Old Testament, then into the heart of a king called Herod who sought to murder the young child Jesus and his mother Mary, Matthew 2:12, 13. Whenever Satan clicked his fingers, Jean ran to meet with him and do his will without question. He blew the trumpet and she rode into battle, throwing caution to the wind.

When the 'accuser of the brethren', Revelation 12:10, thinks he will be found out, he takes on human form. He has no hands but your hands, no feet but your feet, no mouth but your mouth. If you looked into this woman's heart you would see the limited activity of the devil, but if you look into the world at large you will see him as a lion seeking to kill, steal as a thief and destroy, John 10:10. I do not know if Jean was aware of the things that she was allowing to happen in her life or if she was just naive. Whatever Satan called her to do, she did without question and with alacrity. She was his mistress and partner in the crime of character assassination. It was no sooner said than it was done.

Margaret knew that when God created Adam from the soil of the ground, that soil as such did not stay in Adam. He was made into something more beautiful than the mud he was created from. The mud that Jean had been created from was in evidence in her life and she was throwing this mud wherever she went, and sowing seeds in it. The more open she was to evil influences the stronger those influences became. They were as described by Jesus (Matthew 13) as birds of the air, coming, diving, and taking away good seed. The order had been reversed, for Jean was acting like a bird, not to catch the seed away, but to swoop and plant bad seed where it would bring forth a harvest of despair. Hers was the relish of the farmer seeding his soil. That sown would grow up as tares that would destroy the rest of the harvest. The tares would invade the area reserved for the real seed.

The wrong that Jean was doing was not that she was committing murder or robbery in the literal sense, but she had become the tool of Satan when she had been the tool of truth. The order of effort and service had been reversed. Sonship had been turned into prodigal. She was being given seeds to sow that would result in dismay and denial.

Margaret saw a demon following Jean, and the demon was using her as his earthen vessel, as his treasure chest, the place of deposit. Discord was being planted into Jean, and then she was planting what had been sown. It was one of the seven deadly sins, to sow discord among the brethren. Jean felt that she was a free agent, but Margaret was able to tell her that she was not acting alone; she was a special agent of a demon who was trying to influence her. Jean had been tripped up by this evil influence, like begets like, and that copied is repeated. Jean was only doing what had happened to her. Someone, somewhere, who had been hurt, had planted seeds of discord into the heart of this unsuspecting child of God. Jean was taking her pain and giving it to others. If she had been deceived, why shouldn't they be deceived? What had been sown in her spirit, what she had allowed in demon influence, she would influence others with. We water others with the stale water we carry with us. If we are out of tune, we try to get others to sing out of tune. Be alarmed when worry is the best thing you can give to another.

Margaret was talking, and taking an awful risk. If what she was telling Jean was wrong, then she could be accused of misjudging another person. It would have resulted in a slap in the face for her. Yet she knew that what she was telling Jean was correct because the Lord had revealed it to her.

How would Jean respond when being told what was happening to her? Would she throw a tantrum, because she was well known for this skilful manipulation? Would she fly into a rage? Would she come out fighting, denying everything, even her own new birth? All these ploys have been used by Satan throughout the years, but it must come to a stop. Margaret was saying to Jean, 'The buck stops here!' Margaret was prepared to take a risk, if it resulted in someone being rescued from the jaws of the lion. The mark of the beast would be removed as a plague on a soul.

Divinity will always conquer the devious in demons. Margaret knew that the word of the Lord would bring searing conviction into any soul. Like a sword she must use what was available to her. There must be no holding back. If Margaret held back, then she would be an accessory to the fact because the Lord had revealed the whole situation to her, lock, stock and barrel, or head, tail and feet.

As Margaret spoke to the woman, not as one high and mighty, but one clothed with the words in her heart: 'But for the grace of God there go I'. Any gap between Jean and Margaret was closed until they became one in Christ Jesus. Jean began to weep as Margaret began to tell her these things. The emotions she trusted in were flowing away, never to return. The unsure was becoming sure, the unwanted wasted. The more Margaret told her, the deeper the agony and the louder the weeping became, as if the heart of Jean was being opened after it had been shut up like a prison. The key to the cell had been thrown away, but Margaret came with a kingdom key promised to every believer by Jesus Christ, Matthew 16:19; Revelation 1:18. As Margaret spoke, the tool of Satan was set loose and was falling, not to destruction, but another hand would catch it, a gentle, soft, crucified hand. That tool would be something new in the Lord Jesus Christ. The buried talent was being unearthed.

Jean admitted all that was said was true. The revelation had been from the Lord. Jean had been going about sowing mischief among those around her. If she had not agreed with a thing, then she made sure that all knew about it. Worse than that, she had not only been passing on information from one source to another, but was the one who had caused groups to stand aloof. A wedge the size of a seed had been put between people and that had grown to something so big it that could not be denied or measured. Hearts had been hurt by the operations of an evil surgeon, now he was being 'struck off'. Satan's reign had come to an end.

Using anger, viciousness and spite, Jean had sought to cause others not only debate but to destroy. Now she was being set free by the blood of God's Son Jesus Christ, who freely forgave all as she confessed to the Lord what had been done. She could never undo the wrong but she could try again, start again, and see the will of God drawing folk together. God had a new role for her, to make her into a daughter of consolation, where she could bring those apart closer. Never again would she sow seeds of discord, she would sow hope and accord among those in the Church. This was one battle that Satan did not win. His influence was buried that day in the field where the seeds of discord had been sown.

9

THE PROTECTION OF THE HOME

Many weapons are given to us to help in our spiritual walk, talk and warfare. Margaret was not shy when it came to obtaining these weapons or in using them to resist and defeat evil. Although physically weak in body there was within her the spirit of ten men. Some may think that when we use the weapons given to us that are not carnal, but mighty through God to the pulling down of strongholds, 2 Corinthians 10:4, they are heavenly weapons to deal with earthly things, a sort of parable in power. They might also think that these weapons of warfare should only be used in large evangelistic crusades, or when going to the top of a mountain to throw down the power of Satan to the earth. Jesus has already done that when He died on the Cross, Ephesians 4:8. Prior to the cross, He said that He saw Satan fall like lightning from heaven, Luke 10:18. These articles of war are the things you use when facing tremendous odds, or in dire situations, yet they are never seen to be related to home or family life. Why do we draw a line between the secular and the spiritual, between the laity and the professional?

Margaret believed in the supernatural having an influence in the natural world. No line was drawn where God would or would not move. The whole world, latitude and longitude, belonged to the Lord. Every part of the natural creation whether in the sky or on the skyline was part of God's creative activity. He had been the Artist in green and growth, seas, sand and sunshine. Margaret saw it all as coming from the hand of the Lord. God was never a million miles away, He was the God who talked with her, and was alongside every happening in the day. No moment, asleep or awake, was not made sacred to His presence; it was through each mundane thing that the handiwork of the Lord was seen.

God was in the kitchen as much as He was in the pulpit. Every chair in the home was a throne. The home was as much God's property as anything in nature. The music in the home was as sacred as the song of the thrush in the garden. He was as much in the kitchen as in the Kingdom. Everything around Margaret was created and sustained by God; it was where the Lord reigned in majesty. Those who could not see the glory of God in the smile and laughter of a child, a leaf on the tree or the petal of a flower, or are unable to distinguish the multiplicity of God's nature in the many colours of creation, were dull, blind and unable to see afar off. Margaret's eyes were wide open to all that was His, and that included herself and her family.

Home to Margaret was not bricks and mortar, doors and windows with slates on a roof; it was an atmosphere where the Almighty was free to move as He decided. Love was a commodity that all the family required. With the children, nothing was too great or small to take to the Lord in prayer. The challenge was to leave it with the Lord. This prophetess would not go into prayer, and leave only half of the problem with God. From a bee sting to a grazed knee, she would take it and leave it, knowing the Lord would take it. Jesus died so that He might live and be involved in all things. God was in the centre of every happening as One seeking to be acknowledged. This was not just another problem, but God's opportunity to prove Himself. Each problem was lined with glory waiting to be revealed at the right moment.

Ministry to Margaret or 'Marnie' as we used to call her was not just inside a church but outside, not only in the world, but in the cornfields where the daises grew, and in the home where she lived. God's package included all these things. It did not just relate to the public but to the private, and to prayer. Much of what she saw, heard and obeyed was received while on her knees, small, vulnerable, incapable, usable and thankful. This handmaiden of the Lord would be a 'hand' maiden as prayer was uttered. When Margaret fed, raised, washed and clothed her family, these were acts of service that were performed for the Lord. In ministering to her own body, her own children she felt that the Body of Christ was being ministered to. When she left the church, the church did not leave her. God was never left at the altar or in the choir. He continued with her for He was the never ending God. In everything she did there was always the thought that she acted as a priest (bridge builder) for the Lord.

Margaret, while still living with her parents, had gone to a mid-week meeting at the local church. She returned home tired and it seemed as if her spirit had set with the sun. She retired to bed, but first there was a need to pray and read her Bible. Ah! That wonderful book, so wonderful that when she felt knocked off her feet what she read would stand her upright. Margaret felt that what she paid for the Bible was an investment, costing nothing, because the cover alone was worth the price that had been paid. Her belief in the Bible was implicitly simple. Literal in faith and knowing how God felt about her brought everything into the oneness of her spirit as she prayed on this occasion. After reading and prayer it seemed as if the peace of God became her bed sheets, and within moments there was no sound, only the gentleness of a breathing, sleeping saint.

The night seemed to have come to an end suddenly. Margaret was in bed yet wide awake. The abruptness of the moment had suddenly taken all sleep from her weary mind. When she had gone to sleep, everything was as sweet and as neat as the inside of a flower. Now things had changed dramatically, she could feel an evil presence filling the room, as if a hand had been placed over the window during the daytime, and it was dark within while daylight without. It was so real it could be touched. Margaret stepped out of bed, first to the right and then to the left. Then she began to look around to see if the evil presence could be seen. What shape was it? Where was it hiding? Who was it and what was it? Margaret did not believe in ghosts, but she did believe in demons trying to take on human forms to frighten people and to get a hold on their life. This evil power must be controlled, so going down stairs and examining each room, unable to find the evil source, or discover the mind behind this manifestation, she returned to her bedside, not to sleep but to use one of her weapons which was prayer.

As Margaret prayed she felt that every member of the family was in danger. Prayer must be made for each one. That prayer was as deep as it was long, and as strong as it was high. Hell was touched and heaven opened up to her. It was so deeply impressed on her spirit to pray that the blood of Jesus Christ would cover each member of her family. This was no ordinary night prayer from a tired spirit. She had been rejuvenated by the Spirit of the Lord, and it was with strong crying that she prayed. Prayer moved into another realm, the realm of answers received. The family had to be as covered by the blood that Jesus surrendered on the cross as she had been covered while sleeping between the sheets and blankets. As those bedclothes had kept her warm and secure, she felt compelled to pray that her family would be secure by the blood of Jesus Christ. The feeling was so intense that it became more praying. This was intercession, standing in the gap between the family and God. Her parents were religious but had not yet surrendered to Jesus Christ.

Suddenly there was a release in the spirit realm. The storm was calmed, as if Jesus himself had said to the raging sea 'Peace; be still.' (Be muzzled like a dog).

The evil presence disappeared more quickly than it had appeared. The glory of God filled that bedroom as it became the tabernacle of the Almighty. The work of evil had been interrupted, and this night of evil would become the morning of joy. How could evil be overcome so quickly? How could that vice grip of evil suddenly be loosened, that presence of torment given its marching orders? As these thoughts streamed through her head, Margaret fell into a beautiful, natural sleep, the sleep of the just with the peace of God as a guardian angel, Psalm 34:7.

Suddenly it was morning. The light streamed through the bedroom window. This was the day the Lord had made and she must be glad in it and rejoice, Psalm 32:11. Margaret tiptoed down stairs expecting somebody to make a comment about the previous night, for she felt sure that the presence of evil that had been so real must have been felt by others. All that greeted her was a wall of silence. Not a word was spoken, not a feeling was made known, and Margaret felt a little disappointed. Was she the only one who had felt that presence? Shrugging her shoulders she simply began to get her breakfast.

Hiding her disappointment, Margaret went to bed that night. As was her custom she fingered the promises of God and prayed before she fell asleep. When she prayed she felt that the Lord would tell her what it all meant. Margaret began to ask questions and the Lord began to give her the answers. What did that tangible presence of evil mean? Was it the omen of a coming disaster? Was it making a statement of the torment that the evil presence would bring upon that family and their business that they had worked so hard to build up? As Margaret pleaded in prayer she felt that a breakthrough had come. God had answered her prayer, and everything would be alright as the evil presence was dismissed from her mind.

Margaret, in pleading, prayed, asking the Lord what it all meant. Convinced that what God said He meant. 'If you ask a fish I will not give you a serpent, Luke 11:11. 'If you ask for a piece of bread I will not give you a stone.' When God says 'bread', He means bread and He gives bread. Here was food for thought! 'Give us this day our daily bread,' Matthew 6:11. This was daily bread being asked for, but there needed to be some butter on it! As Margaret pleaded before the throne of grace, the Spirit of God said, 'To get an answer to your prayer, ask your father,' (meaning Margaret's earthly father) Silvanus. For some this would have been disappointing. Why didn't Jesus tell her there and then what it all meant? God had a plan, and He was revealing it little by little. He wanted to influence Margaret's parents, wanted them to be involved in what had happened.

Margaret went downstairs, the hour was late, but she was determined to get the answer to her prayer before she went to sleep. 'Is there anything wrong that you have not told me about?' Margaret asked. Her father turned from the television (he had been watching the news), and said, 'I didn't want to trouble any of you, so I did not tell you what happened on the previous night.' Margaret's dad was revealing his own true nature which was one of hiding things and secrecy. 'Let them find out, but I will not tell them' was his motto throughout life.

The Warwicks owned two shops, one a drapery store the other a self-service store and post office. 'Yesterday morning when I went to open the door between the house and the shop, smoke met me, thick black smoke that filled both shops. I could hardly breathe, so I opened the main doors that led out onto the main street, and the smoke bellowed out of the shop. There was smoke everywhere accompanied by the smell of burning.' He told Margaret how he had tried to find the source of the fire. A long thick cable ran through the shops supplying electricity to both. An electrical fire had started at one end of the cable and had gone to the other end, stopping by the shop counter. At the end of the cable was a large cornflakes box that usually contained a dozen smaller cornflake boxes. Margaret's father had emptied the huge box, and used it as a paper bin. The cable burned the outside of the box, leaving a hole as the evidence of its presence, and then it had filled the shops with smoke. Rubbish near the hole was scorched, but the fire had miraculously gone no further. After it reached some waste paper that should have been set alight, it stopped. Fires don't usually do that, for they greedily eat up anything that is before them, particularly paper!

Margaret's father knew something about the power of electricity, and he could not fathom why it had not gone on to burn the waste paper and rubbish in the box. He finished his story with a look of perplexity on his face. There was something here that could not be explained.

Margaret began to tell her parents about the evil presence, and how she had prayed, feeling that the Lord had answered her prayer. Her father, with a look of bewilderment on his face, told her that he knew something had happened to stop the fire. Fire in a cable does not travel to a rubbish bin, filled with paper and then stop. There had to be something else at work, and it was in the home that night. God had proved that He was as interested in a fire in the home as in Pentecostal fire. The hand of the Lord had come across the path of that evil destructive element, and had restricted it, causing it to stop at the very place where the fuel for the fire abounded. Here was the Sovereignty of Jehovah seen in every sphere.

The devil had written his evil work in smoke and flame, but the Eternal had written His testimony in causing the fire to cease at the very spot where it should have spread. Where God stops, the devil must stop. When God's red light comes on, the devil's black light must go off. All spiritual battles are not fought and won in the heavenlies. Good had triumphed over evil. The family and the business had been saved; had evil prevailed there would have been a lot of damage and possible loss of life. God does not answer prayer with smoke, but He can and does make it so that even fire must fade when facing eternal realities.

Margaret felt that when she 'broke through' in prayer the precious blood of Jesus not only negated the evil presence but also put the fire out. It draws a line and none may go over it. Prayer was a weapon that must be used, and when the Lord says, 'So far and no further,' then that is the end of the matter. Margaret felt even snugger as she retired to bed that night knowing that, 'He that keeps Israel neither slumbers nor sleeps,' Psalm 121:3. The evidence of evil was in smoke, while the evidence of the power of God was seen in singed paper. Margaret's father, Silvanus Warwick, knew from experience that fire does not suddenly go out when the conditions are favourable. He knew that something of a spiritual nature had happened that night, serving as a prompter to bring him and his wife to Jesus Christ a few years later. God was adding miracle to miracle after the miraculous conversion of his daughter. It was through such miracles as these that they were brought to faith in Jesus Christ, having witnessed the power of God over electricity, paper and fire.

10

WATCH YOUR STEP!

The Church has been called to be a Christian army. That means it must be well trained, and know how to march in time, each soldier letting discipline go to his feet, as he walks with others. It is folly to be out of step, or it can mean that you are out of touch with another's needs. It was the Lord who taught Ephraim to walk (Hosea 11:3). When meeting with others who are proclaiming Jesus Christ as their Saviour, it is good to see if they walk as He walked, for He has left an example for us to follow, 1 Peter 2:21. We must follow in His footsteps, and if we do we shall arrive where He has arrived and walk where He has walked. The tread is softer when He has been there before, and has made His footprint the measure of your own. That footprint can be the measure of your soul! The depth of the footprint you leave on the sands of time is the measure of your dedication. The promise of Jehovah was that wherever their feet trod, the land would be theirs, Joshua 1:3. When I read that I prayed, 'Lord, give me big feet!'

His footprints are seen in life and through the grave to the right hand of God. Shoes may wear out, but the sureness of the soft landing of the foot is assured if it is placed in the example of Jesus. His footprints are better than slippers, running, climbing or walking boots. Other shoes, efficient and comfortable, might not get you there, but what He is will. That to be followed is always in the ascendancy! To wear His footwear we must have the humility of John Baptist who did not feel worthy to loose the latchet of His sandals, Mark 1:7; John 1:27.

Margaret had compassion for others, and even as a young woman frequently went to visit the sick and widows, so that they might be helped. In this way she was helping them to walk along the Christian pathway to the Eternal day. There was always a sense of the supernatural left when she departed from any dwelling, given in a word of encouragement, or shopping that she had brought for the occupant of the house. The Lord dwelt where she had been. People were left worshipping who had been found worrying. If they had been uneven in their Christian walk, they were onto a straight path, walking in the light from the celestial city.

Susan came towards Margaret, and at first Margaret thought that she had been drinking.

There was a wobble between each step; not that she was off balance, but there was a deliberate act in what she did. The way Susan walked suggested that she was trying to crush spiders or insects, but Margaret could not see anything on the floor. Instead of walking in a straight line, Susan was weaving to the left and right.

Margaret realised that this woman was not incapable, there was no Pentecostal drunkenness in her soul, and each step she took was a deliberate decision. There was no broken glass or pitfall to be avoided. Susan was treading on something that was troubling her, trying to crush that which would crush her. Was Susan treading on burdens and crushing them beneath her feet as Jesus had put Satan under His feet, Ephesians 1:22? Maybe she was treading the tempter down, sending him into hell below, trying to create a pathway for the fallen from earth to hell. Margaret knew that there was no such ministry in the Bible.

There was a glow on the face of Susan that was not the glow of glory. It was the glee of jealousy. The light of a child getting its own way lit her face, and revealed the deep furrows in her forehead. It was the glow of satisfaction for a mission accomplished, the grin of the naughty child lighting her face. If her prayers had been answered, why was she walking as one with uneven heels on her shoes or one leg shorter than the other? If Susan was on a mission of mercy, judging by her actions, and the way she was stamping her feet, there was dedication illustrated in her life. The steps were first one way then the other way, as if Susan was trying to leave footprints in the rock. There was a determination that anyone following her footsteps would be in no doubt where she had been. The holes she would leave behind would not only be deep enough to plant seeds for a harvest, but also deep enough to plant a forest of trees! Margaret had often seen her father, having planted lawn seeds, step onto the surface and stamp his feet to flatten the surface and send the seed into germination.

If anyone wanted an example on how not to walk straight, or to take the longest route from A to B (or should I say A to Z?) then Susan was the one to follow. The way Susan was conducting herself you could tell that she was not climbing a ladder or a mountain, because if she had been doing that she would take three times as long to accomplish what could be accomplished with straight strides. Her movements were like the proverbial dromedary running from side to side.

Margaret began to ponder. Was this a woman with a damaged foot that required healing? If that was so, then the way she was treading would damage the foot more. Had she been born with a twisted foot? What she was doing would not help a foot to heal, but would delay the healing process. Susan did not seem to be walking the talk or talking the walk. We have all heard of those who 'tread where angels fear to tread', but there was no stopping Susan. It seemed as if her brain was out of kilter, and nothing would stop her from doing what was determined, for she was acting like a programmed machine, like one treading grapes, crushing everything under her feet. Margaret began to look for the sweet wine as juice from the grapes, but there was none, only the constant thud of a woman not being led by the Spirit but being led by her feet. It reminded Margaret of the African proverb: 'only a fool tests deep waters with both feet.' 'Your feet will take you anywhere if they have no will or impulse to control them,' thought Margaret. The proverb says, 'Look before you leap', and Susan was looking and leaping, as if the world depended on where her feet were placed.

Then revelation began to emerge as Margaret sought the Lord. The woman was letting her feet do the talking. All she felt had gone from her heart and her brain into her feet. Here was a woman with evil feet, feet that were not doing the work they had been designed to do. The hammer can be used to hammer, the saw to saw, and feet must be used to walk. There is many a stumble between a hop, skip and a jump! At one point Margaret was wondering if she was practising a dance from a voodoo ceremony! There was anger, malice, jealousy and pride in those feet, but Susan was not stamping to get rid of those things, what she was doing was to promote it. Susan wanted to hurt others, using her pain to get her own back on humanity. Margaret pitied anything those feet trod on.

In an old custom, to destroy a king after capturing him you placed your foot on his neck before he died. Susan's feet did not stay in one place long enough for her to promote any other activity, she had been to one place, taken one step, a series of steps that were not taking her anywhere. If Susan was trying to make an impression then there was no failure. You can only walk with others as you have regard for their feelings. Others are not with you to be trodden on. The Lord never intended us to tread with such force that we are capable of sinking a mine shaft as we walk. Susan had received her marching orders. Who was giving the orders? In the New Testament the record states 'the crowd was so great that they trod on one another,' Luke 12:1. We tread on things dear to us when our lives become too crowded.

Susan would have adequately filled the part of 'Man Friday' in Robinson Crusoe's story on a desert island. He realised that a visitor had been on the island when he discovered a footprint! Susan was for burying people alive! These footprints and the treading on others was the initial evidence of a heart that was far from God, a life that was being led not by fear but by feet!

Margaret, in the Spirit of God, began to look closer at those feet. They were not the feet of a fairy, rather the feet of an elephant. The weight would crush a spider or a fly into oblivion. Susan was wearing large riding boots, the sort that a farmer might wear when going into his field to inspect the nature and growth of his crop. Susan's feet were well protected, but those she was treading on were not protected. The boots had strong nails in the soles. They were built to last, blast, blight and smite, instruments of hurt and torture. A light could be put out forever as one of those boots covered the glow worm or the butterfly. Susan was wearing that which would hurt, bruise, crush and destroy, hurting through your feet as you ran 'rough shod' over another, leaving them bleeding and crying.

The size of the boots was enormous, but they fitted this woman's feet, and she was using them as weapons in her warfare. The larger the pain, the greater the feeling of anger, then the larger the boots seemed to grow, for they were weapons of ambition and annihilation. Susan and the boots fitted one another well. The size of the boots told of the steely character that was in this lady. Here was one who was determined to go where she wanted to go, tread wherever she felt led. Her identification mark was in the sole of a boot. Boot first and questions afterwards was her theology! Obviously Susan believed in 'the order of the boot'. If you can't get them to agree with you then tread on them, walk them into the ground until they are small enough to be manipulated. Let fruit fall from the trees and be trodden on until it becomes dirt.

The war was not being waged or directed against the enemy, Satan, but against those who were around Susan as small, tender flowers that could easily be broken. Trouble is to be expected when crowds gather together without leadership, for rows and revivals go together. Walking in the light as He is in the light demands discipline, the discipline of walking carefully. This was not a revival but a row, and Susan was the mother, sister and daughter of it! Through her conduct, with no regard for the feelings of others, she was ploughing through them, using her feet as her plough blades. First this one and then that one was stamped on. If they did not agree with her or said anything she did not appreciate, then she was letting them know how she felt, and in doing so was 'walking all over them'. Her heels bruised their head. Susan was burying folk without using a spade to dig the earth. Using her feet as battering rams she was murderously crushing all opposition into subjection. Saints, God's children were being treated as sparks from hell, and Susan must put out the sparks before they were fanned into a flame. Susan was treading on the lion and the adder, but there was no discernment when she came to the sheep. Buttercup, daisy, flower of note and worth, all were treated as pebbles or broken rock and must be crushed with a curse. It wasn't her literal feet that were being used but the words she spoke which were laced with vinegar. The footprint or boot mark was left embedded on gentle toes and feet. The bruises were the size of the boots that Susan was wearing. There was nothing dainty or darling about this daughter.

Susan felt that if she did not crush others she herself would be crushed. 'They' were the opposition, and needed to be dealt with. The king's edict must be carried out. It was as bad as the 'Queen of Hearts' in *Alice in Wonderland*, who said of everybody 'Off with their heads!' This was 'off with their feet'. Making sure they could not walk and fetch help from afar, they were injured into paralysis. Susan forgot that these people could pray about her and her destructive ways, and they did. Margaret and the revelation she received was an answer to the prayers of these hurting people in the church.

If that surrounding Susan was not controlled, then it would control her. Here in this female was the 'spirit of Jezebel'! Revelation 2:20. Susan had a ministry of hurting others by treading on them and bruising beautiful feet that had been adorned with the gospel. If any of those people had corns or bunions the pain was even greater. Those having difficulty walking the Christian way were turned into cripples and beggars. There was no great shout of fear or pain as she did this, because it was so unexpected. God did not meet like with like, but He sent one of another kind (the meaning of kindness) to help those in distress. There were those who through Susan's evil ministry spent more time on their bottom than on their feet. God does not go to the tributary but to the fountain head in order to deal with anything.

Those around Susan were full of joy and laughter, but through her actions and words (words are wholesome but it depends how we use them and for what purpose); happiness was being turned into hurt; joy was trodden into jangled nerves. Those feet that were beautiful were marked and scarred by unholy conduct. One step from these shoes, and the light went out as you sank below the ground. Instead of the saintly nature being promoted, it was destroyed. The reed was bruised until it became something else. (Matthew 12:20)

In Susan's mind was the thought that if she trod hard enough, speaking her mind, then that which was sweet, kind and Christ-like would grow from a crushed seed into something like herself. Susan was using army boots when treading on the silk of sainthood. Kind begets kind, and what she was sowing would be reaped. It could have helped if a large notice was placed near Susan that said, 'Do not walk on the flowers!' Here was control in its strongest form coming from a woman. People were being driven as a butcher might drive sheep to the slaughterhouse; Margaret was looking for the Shepherd of the sheep to come to their rescue.

As Margaret began to pray for Susan her feet walking ceased, as if she had been sleep walking and was awakened by the morning light. This was no morning light; it was the love of the Lord encased in bright shining light. Each word spoken was a word of light and penetration. The tears began to flow; the evil footprints disappeared, as this woman's tears caused a rainbow to appear over a valley of distress. These were not tiny tears but tears that were washing the torment away, forever and a day. That which was schizophrenic was being restored to the rest of the body. God was taking off those heavy, muddy, mountaineering boots, to give her something that would help Susan walk in the right way. God had to deal with her heart and hurt before He dealt with her feet. That had to be reconciled to His control. As Susan surrendered, Margaret saw the Lord take off His sandals, the sandals of the Son and Servant, Jesus Christ, and put them on to the feet of Susan. The remarkable thing was, they fitted perfectly.

Instead of walking all over others, Susan made footprints gently that led to the homes of those she had hurt. The new footprints were the shape of the feet of Jesus Christ, and could be followed from time into eternity, without the follower being injured, or feeling that if they followed they would be with the Good Samaritan, fall among thieves. These were ministry shoes, not misery shoes. Susan felt as Cinderella did in the children's story, as her torn shoes turned into golden slippers to be worn by a princess. Moses was commanded to take his shoes off his feet, and the Almighty could give him that which enabled him to face and walk heavenward. Susan could now make progress in the right direction with the right motives. She would use her God-given shoes to walk the talk, to minister unto and into hurting people. These footprints were worth following, for they would lead upward and onward, not downward to hell, but to heaven. They would display some of that 'all glorious within' that had entered into the King's daughter, Psalm 45:13.

The look on Susan's face was the look of immense pleasure, as if she had been taken around a clothes store, and at somebody else's expense clothed in new garments and shoes. She now felt fully dressed and not depressed. It is amazing what a pair of new shoes will do for a woman! Walking in Christ's sandals she would be expected to do the work of Jesus Christ, to lift people up. Jesus would never hurt, He would only heal, and Susan must do the same.

11

DESTRUCTIVE DEPRESSION

Depression is an awful thing. It was described by Sir Winston Churchill as his 'Black Dog'. It can take the shape of a shadow that passes across the mind, or seems as if the curtains have been drawn over the windows leaving the beautiful sunshine outside. There appears be no hand to draw the curtains back, and allow the glory of the sun and sky to enter into the prison of the mind. Who can conquer this feeling of despair? To some it is utter despair that comes upon them when they least expect it. There always seems to be that substituting blessing which can be defined as cursing. The song of life should be a serenade that song can end in silence and blackness. Occasionally something dramatic triggers depression, but at other times it just seems to happen. Depression can lead to suicide as it distorts your thinking, believing nobody cares and nothing matters.

It was at times like this that Margaret would turn to 1 Peter 5:7 'Cast all your care on Him, because it matters to Him about you.' The verse seemed to send the honey of Canaan into her soul. Casting her care upon Him, because He cares enough not to worry in your worry. The word 'cast' is used in the New Testament of 'casting' clothes over the back of the donkey Jesus was to ride on, Luke 19:35. In a beautiful turn of phrase it describes sick people being laid gently at the feet of Jesus Christ, Mark 6:56; feet will tread the tempter down, crushing the dynasty of depression, ensuring that every valley, every low feeling, is filled with the glory of God. Those sitting in darkness begin to see a great light, the dawning of a new day. The darkest hour has passed into oblivion. For Margaret, after a time of seeking the Lord, the singing of the birds had come. There was a fresh discovery that she could do all things through Christ who strengthened her. Mountains were turned into molehills, valleys into grains of sand that the wind of the Spirit could blow away.

For some it seems as if an iron cage has suddenly been placed around their head, they have become a person in an iron mask. For those who experience depression there appears to be no future, only a sad present. Every slight jolt becomes a hammer blow as things weigh heavy on the spirit.

All depression is not demon possession or oppression, yet for some people it can be. It can also be the result of being 'run down' because you have thought that caring for the world was your ministry. The work in hand can become too large for you to handle. You feel like a smashed vessel with all the contents of your heart being splashed all over the place. There can also be a normal medical explanation for people in depression. It is as if their mind had closed down. You can feel that tomorrow has been cancelled because of the lack of interest. There is no future when you suffer with depression, no way out, only a way into deeper suffering with no one to help. You can cry and shout, but unless you pray it seems as if there is no one to dry your tears, and you are left alone to suffer what life pours upon you. It is to be in a dark, icy sea with no shoreline or bottom.

No one has all the answers to depression; it is a malady that holds no melody for some. It can feel as if the strings of the string instrument have suddenly become loose without snapping. What was once a beautiful melody has now become just misery. All the music is in the minor key, and it is the heart with the funeral dirge instead of the wedding ceremony.

A child was trying to sew a pattern on a piece of cloth, but she kept sticking the needle into her hands. The voice of the teacher was heard to say 'Keep on working at it, and the rose will appear.' The child could only see holes and wool, a shadowy pattern, yet as she continued the rose appeared and made it worth all the effort.

There are those who can offer help. One of the main healing streams is that which comes to us in quietness and confidence as we wait upon the Lord, Isaiah 30:15. In that waiting we take on the position of weakness. The figure of a sick person before the physician is brought to us. We have been promised that if we 'wait on the Lord' we shall be 'renewed' — to 'exchange strength'. The way some people act and react is a token of their mood that has swung right off the instrument that measures mood swings. There is a balm in Gilead, found in Jesus Christ, which is better than the finest medication that ever came from Gilead and its mountainous region. You have to spend and spend to obtain some ointments but the ointment poured forth in the name of Jesus is spread over the hurt, Song of Solomon 1:3. Sometimes healing does not come from a prescription handed in at a pharmacy, it comes from many sources. The whole programme and process is one of 'waiting'. 'In waiting I waited, I waited, I waited' said the psalmist, Psalm 40:1. The Chinese have a beautiful saying, 'I am waiting for my soul to catch up with my body.' The Japanese translation of Psalm 23:1 is 'The Lord is my pacesetter.' Margaret sometimes felt out of kilter, her only response to slow down, and allow that which was disjointed to come back together again as found in Ephesians 4:12, where it speaks of the 'perfecting' of the saints, meaning putting a dislocated joint back together again.

Margaret had occasionally suffered from depression, and experiencing something yourself then you can empathise with others in their suffering. Birds build nests on branches they have visited previously. There will always be the triumph of the crucified. Margaret never ministered whilst in a depression in case she depressed others. At times it was as if she was scraping the bottom of her heart, and there was nothing to give. Terry, her husband, had once had a vision of a church with members like wounded soldiers. Some had eye patches, some bandages, plasters, and each looked like a walking medicine chest or first aid kit! These church members were symptom swapping, taking plasters and bandages, and giving them to each other, and diseases were spreading like a plague. They were finding comfort, not healing, in one another's hurts and pains.

Margaret knew if you feed faith and starve doubts, then those doubts would die. Her ministry was to emphasise all the positive things in the Christian life. If she fell into a lake of milk, she knew that to keep swimming would turn it into cheese, and then she could step on it, and get out! Some things do not come in dreams or rainbows, they come through broken spirits. When visiting those in depression, Margaret always took the negative and turned it into a positive. Midnight became midday. Sunbeam became sunray, as the Son of Righteousness rose with healing in His wings. Depression may be one thing to one person, but God has a thousand ways to deal with it. God would take Margaret and use her to see a young man delivered.

The equipment and ministry came through her own suffering. If another had a need, she had been where the need was. Taking all influences, good, evil, kind or unkind, bitter and sweet there was the ability to twist together and form them into a rope that could be lowered into another's dungeon. Where there was a place where grace had been, it would be taken there in the hands of this servant of the Lord.

Margaret never dwelt in an 'ivory palace'. There was nothing aloof or far removed in her life. Her ministry was with the vacuum cleaner and where the brush and shovel had its own place. To her, every thing, no matter how small or menial, was part of the kingdom of God. When every day was everyday, it was another opportunity to serve the Lord of glory. Having raised three children, and with four teenage grandchildren, she was one with humanity in every aspect. When saints who were sad went to her it was to be embraced, understood and prayed for.

She spent much time on the telephone praying for those who had a need. That telephone became a pill dispenser. It was the heart of the Great Physician. Margaret had a wonderful way of opening up a life as the Lord opened the heart of Dorcas, like a flower opening up to the sunshine. Every experience had to be treated with respect; you never knew when you might be called upon to use that experience to help another counter the attack of Satan. To those who were unbalanced, she would right them with a promise from the Word of God. Those who were sinking, she sought to leave them singing. Those who came to her in depression, she left without a doubt or fear, wondering why they had ever been depressed. Where black lines had been painted, they were turned into silver lines that resulted in the whole life being re-drawn by the Saviour's hand. Who can resist the hand of the one who suffered so on a cross? In that 'muddy' world of depression, the servant of the Lord would find pearls to help the sufferer.

Whenever Margaret experienced depression, it did not stop her believing or trusting. When she felt depressed, she requested prayer, and through prayer and waiting on the Lord, using her 'other tongue' that God had given her in the baptism of the Holy Spirit, she would ascend back to her position of reigning in life by Jesus Christ. As Margaret spoke in other tongues, the Spirit of God would lift her spirit into another realm, away from the cobwebs of her mind. Time is a great healer, but not greater than God. Margaret knew that time had a healing hand. Sometimes we have to wait, as the yolk within the egg, until the whole is hatched out into a beautiful golden chicken. When we see that happen we know it has been worth waiting for. A pinch of experience is worth more than a ton of speculation or education. Armed with experience, Margaret never lacked conviction that God would bring light from darkness.

The young man looked healthy, wealthy and strong, with red rosy cheeks and hair as black as midnight. Looks are not only deceptive, they can be devilish and a denial of the contents of the heart. From outward appearance this youth looked strong enough to turn back the incoming tide, yet proved to be as weak as a raindrop falling into the sea.

Margaret might have thought she was in a Roman Catholic Church, because she could see in the Spirit a young man in front of her wearing what looked like a halo. There might have been the temptation in her heart to bow low before such a well mannered and dressed young man. Not many living people wear halos; they are usually seen in paintings and drawings of New Testament saints. There would be no yielding to worshiping the saint or angels. That which was around the head seemed like a halo, but on closer inspection she saw it was a crowd of bees, so close together they formed a ring of steel. These bees were neither bringing or producing honey, but hurt and pain, as bee stings would. George was being pained in his mind. The battle for his life was being fought and lost in the area of the mind.

This army of aliens must be conquered. Any halo must be the clothing of the Spirit of the Lord as found in Luke 24:49. God never defeats evil or demonic influence without replacing it with far more. The sorrow He replaces with a song, the weak with the strong. Margaret had thought it was a halo, and then the thought entered into her spirit that they were bees, but that did not seem right. Bees in a church meeting would frighten the timid and drive away those of a fearful and fainthearted disposition. Then the Spirit of God revealed that these were a circle of demons, using this young man's head as an altar, pouring out their woeful songs of spite and hate as they encircled his head. This maypole dance must be stopped for the dance was devoted to the devil!

There was an authority in the heart of the maiden of the Lord that must be used. What use is costly perfume if we continue to inhale foul smells? The promises of the Lord must be believed and acted upon. With a firmer voice and a forceful promise from God Margaret quoted from the Bible. At the mention of the name of Jesus Christ, the circle became a line of broken bits that fell to the ground. Each enemy seemed to have been shot by an invisible ray. The name of Jesus produced such power that they rolled on the floor as mortally wounded soldiers of the deep. These demons seemed as straws in the wind, their power broken in a moment of faith, crushed by a Crucified Hand.

Wherever there are bees there is honey. Samson discovered honey in the carcase of a lion, and would not the Lord provide honey in the carcase of this temptation? Judges 14:8. Temptation was overcome, the honey would be found, and the sweetness of salvation would be restored.

In place of bees and demons a crown of gold was placed upon the young man's head as a sign that he was the son of a King, not just any king, but the King of kings and the Lord of lords. He was free at last, the power of the enemy broken, he was clothed and in his right mind, a mind that could think and act freely. That stolen and conquered was given back to its rightful owner. Instead of the squeaking of demons in their low pitch voices, or the buzzing of bees, the songs of Zion, of the soul set free became part of this young man. A halo of help enriched his heart and life.

God brought into his life that which would produce honey, rich and rare from the highlands of Canaan, honey that was promised with milk in the Land of Promise and through faith. The bees had gone but the true 'buzz' had come. Noise had been conquered and converted into newness of life in Jesus Christ. Going around in a circle was broken, and a straight pathway and a narrow way was before him. He walked on that path as a pilgrim with a shining face. The Lord was now illuminating each step before him so he would not stumble or fall.

12

DISTINGUISHING BETWEEN THE DIVINE AND THE DEMONIC

Many times those things the Lord wants to accomplish for our good, have been taken and used by Satan to turn joy into mourning and light into night. That happens because of the twist in the snake, representing Satan and his kingdom (Genesis 3:1, 2, 4).

I need to remind you that the collective name for demons, the servants of Satan is 'one who does harm'. It only seems to be that way. In truth and reality God always has the last laugh, and He that laughs last laughs longest. Heaven will be one eternal laugh and smile of Almighty God. Psalm 2:4 reveals a laughing God. Who will be the winner at the end of the race? He measures the pace to the size of the saint's foot. Nothing is expected that you are incapable of achieving. It might seem as if runners in the race are behind the rest, but at the finishing tape, God will be there welcoming those who have been delayed but not denied, late but better late than never. The God who brought you in will take you through, and take you up (1 Thessalonians 4:16, 17).

In the Garden of Eden, what God introduced for the good of our forefathers was turned with a twist of the snake's tail into something else. It became blight instead of blessing, but the Lord did not mean it to be like that. God always arranges things for our good, but if that which is bad, like the grub in the apple, appears, be assured that demons have been at work under cover of darkness. We require that spirit of discernment to discern between right and wrong. We need a deep insight into the activities that take place in the lives of others, 1 Corinthians 12:10. We must name it and shame it! See what is happening and put a true estimation on it. Is it a real flower or one of silk? When they presented to King Solomon two lots of flowers, he was asked to judge which were real and which were carved in stone. One was false, one was real, and he had to decide which was which. From a distance it was impossible to tell. Then Solomon said, 'Release the bees!' The bees went immediately to the real flowers to gather nectar.

When Jesus was born, it was a time of rejoicing, but Satan, using the men of this world had babies aged less than two years destroyed by Roman swords, Matthew 2:16. When there should have been singing and dancing, joy and angel choirs, as there had been at the annunciation of the birth of Jesus Christ, Luke 2:13, there had to be the cruel and wasteful side accomplished by the hordes of demons acting out the commands of Satan. While Christians move in ones, demons move as a mighty army seeking to conquer, pillage and destroy all before them.

God does not let Satan have all his own way, or even sometimes, any of his own way. God puts His foot down, and that becomes the end and limit of satanic activity in any life. The cross of Christ becomes the fence and final step for evil. Before we can deal with evil and satanic activity it must be perceived, disarmed because of the Name of Jesus Christ.

Margaret has had many battles with Satan in her own life with constant sickness, and in the lives of others presented to her. People often telephone her morning noon and night asking for prayer. That telephone became a dispensary of things bright and beautiful. One young man, built like the Seven Hills of Rome asked her to pray for him.

Arthur was a believer. He was experiencing depression, and did not know why he felt so depressed. He did not feel that he had sinned or moved outside of the will of God, but something had brought a cloud and a clout to his life that was threatening his sanity. It was something he could not get rid of; it was a torment morning, noon and night, as if part of hell had been established in his mind. There was a fiery disposition of torment in his life.

Arthur was married with two children, and the family depended on him. At the moment he felt dejected and rejected. Instead of his thoughts lifting him up they were dragging him down, anchors rather than sails! Thoughts were coming into his mind faster than tracer bullets. There was no respite night or day for him. With Job it seemed as if night had merged into day, and the day of death was better than the day of birth (Job 3:1–3). Arthur asked Margaret to pray for him, and the Lord, as always, graciously gave Margaret something for him. Many hours were spent seeking the mind of the Lord. It was His mind that made things matter. That real needed to be revealed. Maybe the Lord would help her again with this needy soul? Nothing was taken for granted; no request was treated as a quest without responsibility.

Arthur required more than vinegar and brown paper to be wrapped around his hurting head. He required something that would break his thought patterns. The hand patting the head, and being told to 'snap out of it!' would neither heal nor help this soul in distress. No medicine bottle or pill would help; no prescription pad was large enough to prescribe a cure.

It was Jesus who left a tormented man clothed

and in his right mind (Luke 8:35). When Jesus deals with any person it is body, soul and spirit, and this includes the area of the mind. The mind of this young man was a minefield and a battlefield, he was constantly being shot at, the aim was true finding its mark in his flesh. He had a thorn in the flesh, 2 Corinthians 12:7. He lived night and day in torment, yet there was nothing wrong with his life, wife, marriage or children. The horror of darkness seemed to be all around him.

Margaret felt she must find out from the living God what it was that tormented this young man and his family. Whatever it was must be as a hatched buried, buried so deep that a sign should be put where it was buried: 'No digging here!' Margaret began groaning in her spirit that could not be uttered in any language known in this world, Romans 8:26. As she pleaded before God, a picture of Arthur began to emerge. She opened her heart wide, and God began to paint a picture in it with the colours of grace. God added one part of the picture then another, and it was like turning over the pages of a book. God was revealing a picture book of Arthur's life. As Margaret received first one thing and then another from the Lord, she began to understand why this young, go ahead man was feeling so depressed. This was no revelation in a parable, but each picture and object was crisp as it was clear.

A spirit of righteous indignation began to

well up within Margaret's heart as she saw and understood. 'An enemy has done this,' she said. Why was Satan allowed to influence this young man in such a way? There seemed to be no answer from heaven, only the pictures of a life that was in sore distress. No wonder the young man's head was in a spin!

As Margaret prayed, she could see Arthur in the distance, climbing a steep hill. This figured, for his experience had not been an easy one. Here he was climbing hills that had been so difficult, more difficult than climbing the Seven Hills of Rome. They were making him sweat. Then Margaret saw something that startled her. Arthur seemed to be wearing a halo of glory. Often Margaret had seen in artists' impressions, paintings and drawings of pictures of Jesus and the saints with a halo around their head, albeit they were but figments of the artists' imaginations. What she was now seeing was real. Had she been wrong in thinking that saints do not have halos of glory around their heads? If what she was viewing was true, why was this man suffering such magnitude of depression?

She began to pray a little more, and as she prayed she could see more clearly what Arthur had around his head. It could have been mistaken for a bandage, and maybe that would have helped his healing. Each word uttered in prayer made the picture clearer, as if a mirror was being polished with a cloth. The one wearing a halo came closer to her, so she could inspect it as only a woman can inspect a scene, noting colours, shapes, shades, sizes, how many; was the sky blue or overcast? Things like this women note when they are describing an event.

Margaret, gasping, saw clearly what was around his head. From the distance it had seemed to be something else. Often she had driven along a dark lane at night, thinking she could see a fox in the hedgerow, but, on arriving where she thought it was, discovered it was a piece of paper blowing in the wind. On a dark country lane she thought she saw a man standing in the middle of a field, only to find out in the morning light that it was a scarecrow! Margaret wanted to make sure; she prayed until the figure of Arthur came so close she could see what this halo was. She gasped in horror; it was not what it seemed to be from a distance. It was something entirely different.

Margaret could hear the distinctive sound of bees, many of them buzzing as they flew around in a circle. She turned to see if there were any flowers or bee hives close by. If there were bees here, then there must be flowers. Margaret knew that honey was a sign of prosperity, because God had promised Israel a land that flowed with milk and honey, Exodus 3:8, 17. Samson had taken honey from the carcase of a lion, Judges 14:9. Jonathon's eyes had been lightened by the taste of honey, 1 Samuel 14:25,26. Surely honey and bees could not make a man ill. Margaret knew if you ate too much of any good thing it could make you sick. One of her children had eaten too much chocolate one Easter, and it made her sick. Was it bees and too much honey that was making Arthur sick unto death, and in constant depression?

This was a mystery being unfolded in prayer. Margaret had become a detective in her spirit. Here was a New Testament sleuth, looking for clues, trying to gather evidence, and then bring about a prosecution. Who or what would stand in the dock? What was the source of these bees that were buzzing around the head of Arthur, as if they had an eternal attachment to him? Margaret realised this was an attack of the devil. There was no honey here, only horror and harshness.

The halo she had seen in the distance was not a halo at all. It had appeared as a white form of mist, a bit like the aurora that appears around the moon. This was a pretend thing. Margaret felt she had been deceived. He was something being dressed up appearing in one form but was really something else. It was part of an ambush, put around this young man to bring him to grief. What was making the figure of a halo was a ring of demons that looked, sounded and acted as bees on a mission. They were busy buzzing, but the honey they were seeking was the sweetness of the pleasure of obeying the commands of their leader. These were not seeking honey, but were applying vinegar in the shape of fears and doubts into this young man's mind. The official record says, when anyone commits suicide: 'The balance of their mind was disturbed.' Disturbed by what and whom? It is Satan that puts so many burdens on the mind that it becomes unbalanced, as a see-saw with too much weight on one side.

Margaret must go on the attack, disturb the disturber and attack the attacker. This evil must be broken. Unlike the love of God which is a complete circle, this was not complete. It stayed as it was because the greedy appetite of the bees is to obey every command. There are times during preparation for migration that flocks of birds will form patterns in the sky as they move one way and another.

These bees loved the command of their leader so much it gave them 'a buzz'! These were not honey bees; they were bees with just a sting and no honey, more like hornets. It amazed Margaret that without any honey, they could be such a strong force. They were as those that act to keep intruders away from the hive, they were just drones, planted there to keep people away from the truth and realising what was happening to this young man. He might have been described as having 'bees in his bonnet', and that would have been so true. These bees were meant to sting if you went to the aid and head of Arthur.

Not everybody who suffers depression is under attack from demons. They can have oppression, depression and obsession without it being demon possession. This was an outward influence affecting the inner spirit of the young man. It had nothing to do with what was in him, but was connected and controlled by things around him. These bees would never be found among flowers.

The reason some suffer from depression and mental illness might be medical, a lack of vitamins and other such minerals. In this case it was a direct attack from the enemy who was encircling the young man with what looked like a crown, but was acting as an iron band crushing his brain and his mind out of existence. No wonder his head was in a constant spin as the bees flew round him. Watching them would make you dizzy, and put you into a spin. These were no bees, they were small demons shaped as bees, pretending in hypocrisy to be honey bearing bees when they were not. They had taken on another form to try and influence a human form. They were there to swarm and kill; Margaret must warn and kill the bad influence. They acted as an external force to drive this young man to the verge of suicide.

Immediately Margaret prayed for him, the bees flew away, as if a strong Pentecostal wind had propelled them into the distance. The 'sound of a mighty rushing wind, Acts 2:2, began to chase them away. They could not stand the sound and words of her prayer that had been dipped in the precious blood of Jesus Christ. They did not all blow away at once, for it seemed as if this blowing wind dealt with one after another, commanding them into oblivion. They did not go away together as a circle, but one at a time as they were dealt a death blow. It was as if the summer had been removed from them, and the cold blast of wind sent them into a stupor from which there was no recovery.

What had been present now moved into the future. Arthur's brain began to clear. The fuzzy feeling broke into a clear day. The bees and the sting had been removed, and Arthur could move on in life. The depression lifted; it was morning married to summer time in his heart. His life took on a new meaning. What had been as tinnitus disappeared as sweet music entered into his soul. Honey could never come through goading Arthur to more activity. The sweet taste of salvation began to fill his mouth. His brain was no longer addled, but was calm and composed, as truth honey came from truth that was so sweet after months of torment. In his heart the words sounded as a trumpet call 'Oh, taste and see that the Lord is good,' Psalm 34:8.

It was with a cleansed heart and a clear head that Arthur moved away, his brain as calm as the sea Jesus had calmed, Mark 4:39. The depression had gone; the prisoner had been set free. Prayer had been the key to open the prison. God had done it, letting the mind that was in Christ Jesus rest in this man, Philippians 2:5. There is honey in humility. Here was the same man but different, as different as the sun is to shade. He now had a smile that could not be measured. He walked, gaining feet. He could walk tall without having his head in the clouds. He had a reason to exist and to live.

13

THE HEALING OF
A SPLIT CHURCH

People had left this particular church. Leaving one church for another, people are defined as travellers, but when they leave a church and come to your church they are described as converts. The sheep had been scattered, and not having a shepherd, many had gone their own way.

There was a spirit of discouragement at the altar. It fitted neatly into each chair as if it had been a prodigal returning home, and had found its home. This situation was where it could be ministered into, because through their experience the people had become evangelists in discouragement, their delight being to spread abroad the gloom, doom and hurt that they felt. The atmosphere was heavy because heavy hearts were breathing into it.

Entering the church was rather like going into the blackness of hell without the fire. They were stumbling along, because their reason for existence had been removed. The people were bowing low, but not in worship, but because they felt lower than the floor that they were walking on.

Here was a battlefield, and the atmosphere was one after a war has subsided. Yet these sufferers were not on the victory side. There was no flag flying or trumpet sounding to describe a jubilee. It was the medical wing of the army where soldiers are dying, moaning and groaning because the battle fought had been lost. Here was the arena of tears, blood and sweat without a victory. It had all gone horribly wrong. They felt that their cause was the right cause. None were looking to the future, they were staring at the wounds, and no healing salve was being applied.

Where now was the physician? Instead of looking forward, upward, onward, they were looking at the present. While you look at the present you will never see the future. There was no future. The lame and the sick were looking at the lame and the sick, but God had a plan for their pain, a miracle for their malady.

Some of the members could not decide whether to stay or to go. They were left in doubt — one foot on the earth and one in a boat as the boat moves away from the pier. They were living in a wobble, unable to go one way or another. Indecision is a killer of spiritual appetite, and it closes the mind to future vision. It is so stressful when you are moving from one house to another, and the contracts have not been signed or exchanged. They felt they were being pulled this way and that way with tremendous force. Their plans were as broken eggshells at their feet, feet that would neither go backward nor forward. How could they travel on when they had been left bleeding and dying as the man in the story of the Good Samaritan, Luke 10:30? They were on the Jericho Road, hurting and miserable. The heart yearned from the hurt for a Good Samaritan. Misery was on their faces, as tangible as an orange in the hand.

They were in the position of 'between the devil and the deep blue sea'. They had to be careful that they were not dragged into the deep blue sea without a boat, sail, engine, compass or a rudder. What had been light, love and cheer had degenerated into the gloom of a dark night on a farmyard. It was a question of 'to go or not to go?'

The church had been hurt, as badly hurt as the lion that Samson took hold of and torn limb from limb, Judges 14:5,6. Even in that carcase of the lion, honey would be found, and new things would abound in this church. God never leaves us where He finds us. No man has ever been brought into new life through a wagging finger, only by an outstretched hand, seen on the cross of Jesus Christ. Salvation would still retain its sweetness, even if sedition produce sourness instead of saintliness and sanity.

The Lord gave Margaret a word picture in that she saw what had happened, and in that picture there was not only encouragement for any budding farmer and planter, but the seeds of a new awakening that would restore unto the church what the thief and robber had destroyed. One picture is better than a thousand words. The picture is the orator that speaks with a silver tongue to us. This picture revealed what human nature would plant and produce if not restrained.

Trees appeared in the church through the Spirit of God, as if each wooden pew had grown into a tree. The pews were many and the trees were many. The trees were as many, a veritable forest. It appeared as if there had been a storm of unprecedented equal. Something had taken the branches and tossed them around as spears without a target, each tree had been torn from limb from limb. The leaves had gone; the autumn had come and there was no fruit on the branches. It was a worse picture than that of a deep winter. If winter comes, at least there is hope of new growth in the spring. There was no hope here; it was the valley of despair. It looked like the picture that Jeremiah saw when the fields were empty, and the stalls had no cattle in them, Lamentations 4:9. Yet, in spite of all he saw he still wrote: 'Great is your faithfulness, Lord, unto me,' Lamentations 3:23. Without God the whole thing was miserable, wretched, poor and blind. It seemed as if Pandora's Box had opened, and a storm had been released to do its worst. It had certainly done a thorough work, reaping where it had not sown, and destroying what it had mercilessly stolen from others.

There seemed to be more broken wood than there were trees. The whole thing was a disorganised mess, as if someone had not been cutting down the trees with an axe. Instead of clean cuts and marks, it was as if a strong wind had torn root, bark and branch. This was not the work of the axe but of the wild nature. Each branch was split into many parts. If Zaccheus had been on one of these branches he would have been thrown to the ground and killed, Luke 19:5. Each branch seemed to have been flung far and wide. The receiver of the picture began to wonder what it all meant.

As the picture took shape, the whole scene began to change. A cloud of glory began to ascend from the ground to the trees, and each tree with its broken branch and bared bark was surrounded in glory, glory which appeared from the roots of the broken trees. It was if the Lord of all glory was forming a pattern. Each tree had its own circle, its own crown of glory. The glory did not stay at the bottom branch, but began to ascend from the roots to the top of the trees. It filled all the missing parts. The broken sticks and bits were filled with glory. Where the bark and leaves had been torn from the tree, glory began to fill these areas. God was building as a Gardener, and instead of soil He was using glory! This glory covered everything with the light of the glory of God, as a white dress might cover a bride ready for marriage. God in glory was rectifying every part. Each thing was being moulded in glory.

As the glory ascended and began to thicken, so the roots, broken branches and torn parts began to disappear into the shroud of glory. Then a remarkable thing took place: the glory began to produce new green shoots. The emphasis was not on the old, gnarled, broken trees, but on the new shape of things to come that were appearing as if springtime had arrived on the battlefield. Death and disaster was suddenly represented by new birth. Here was greenery as green as heaven itself. The green pastures of Psalm 23 had been taken and transported to this place, wrapped in glory.

Healing began to take place where there had been hurt and pain. The new looked so beautiful in comparison with the old. The old was lying there, while the new grew upwards in shoot form, as if they were reaching to touch an unseen face. The new growth and expectation of the future was not in dead trees or those that had been uprooted but in the glory of God.

This new growth began to take over until the scene was carpeted in Lincoln green, the transformation taking place before Margaret's eyes. She felt she was witnessing a miracle of the first and last order. Everything was responding to this glory. What had been an 'eyesore' suddenly became a sight worth seeing, a holiday in one glimpse, and the eighth wonder of the world! The glory was spreading everywhere. In fact the green shoots grew where the glory had been. The basis of it all was the glory, and the magnificence of it was the green shoots that began to grow. Here was something produced by that cloud of glory going somewhere and doing something. It did not have to be coaxed or lifted, it just grew and grew, the more growth the more glory. The growth did not diminish the glory, but became a crown sent from the Lord. The dead branches needed to be lifted and removed, for they were only good for burning, but not this new growth. In it was a pattern of things to come. Each green shoot on a mission.

This recovery was not organised and presented in a programme. It came from the roots and its mission was to take everything upward, forward and onward. Everything birthed and clothed was to come from and out of the glory of the Lord. Where the glory had been there would growth be found. The new converts would be sustained and grow up in the glory of God. They could rely on His grace to sustain them through drought and desert, through sunshine and heat, taking them above and beyond the old and the distorted. The new green would out-measure all that had been formal and old, as formal as a dead branch!

God, the God of all glory who Stephen spoke of in the Acts of the Apostles, was visiting this church with His healing power. It was the nature of God, that nature in Jesus Christ, that would be responsible for the vine going over the wall. Genesis 49:22. The glory must come first and then growth would follow. Where the glory went, the new green shoots followed. This growth would remain because it was seeded in the glory of the Lord. It would cover this church as the waters cover the sea, Isaiah 11:9. The scene would be totally changed because of the glory. An artist would use paint and canvas, but the Lord would use glory to depict a new scene as part of a new creation. This would be no stagnant drawing but a living, moving, embracing experience.

If an artist had replaced the trees by painting a seaside scene, it would have been so dull when compared with what the Spirit of the Lord would do. When the Lord changes anything, He does it to better it in every way. You may plant a seed, but it is the Lord who transforms it in one word of promise. Where there had been brokenness there would be wholeness. That which had been torn would be healed. This glory would not restore the old, worn out tree, but there would be new saplings, planted by the Lord, and as in Psalm 1:3 they would be as those planted by a river, their leaves would not wither, and whatever they did would prosper. This was a delightsome land — Buelah.

Margaret passed this on to the minister of the

church, who was delighted with what the Lord had revealed. Margaret was so blessed, because when she had entered that church it had been like the after effects of a great earthquake, but now, through the Spirit of God, everything was to be restored. Not to its former glory, but by the glory of God.

If you are to have change that is not organised, change that will outlast time, sense and reason, it must come through the Spirit of God moving, sometimes in a mist of glory, at other times as a dove, or even as a roaring fire. This move was to be of a gentle nature, as gentle as the wool on the back of a sheep.

14

LIQUID PRAYERS

Susan had a great need, yet she realised that the need was not greater than God. There had been a struggle in her heart as real as Jacob and Esau wrestling in the womb of Rebecca, Genesis 25:22–26, wrestling that continued throughout the life of Jacob, Genesis 32:24,25. That same wrestling spirit had gripped the spirit of this young woman.

In prayer Susan used all the wrestling holds she knew of. The apostle Paul described prayer as a conflict (agony) — the wrestler in the ring using his many holds to pin the opponent down, 1 Timothy 6:12, Philippians 1:30. Susan had read this, and came to the conclusion that prayer was a conflict in which she must wrestle with the Almighty until He yielded. The whole purpose of prayer is to get us to yield to the Father and not the Father to yield unto us. When we yield we are ready to serve, sail, work and win.

Susan was a deep student of the word of God. The promises belonged to her as if to no other, verse, chapter and line. She was an inheritor of great promises of God. That voice was in every promise, the same voice that mustered stars and angels together, and set clouds scurrying on their way before a driving wind, and each raindrop was counted.

She treated the Bible as if it was written just for her, yet despite her pleading, praying asking and seeking, it felt as if dumbness was her companion when prayer was offered. There were times when her prayers seemed to bounce right back off the ceiling of the prayer room. These were boomerang prayers. There seemed to be a piece of elastic on the end of each prayer that kept it coming back as if had not been sent.

A dilemma began to wind itself around her heart. Why didn't God answer her prayers? The word of the Lord was not only believed, it became part of her in her caring, sharing and loving. There were times when in her heart she held court, and sent herself into the witness box to be cross-examined as to why her prayers were not being answered. Were they not frequent enough, were they not fiery enough? Did they lack feeling? If more passion was desired by her Lord and heavenly Father then could He be asked for it? This handmaiden of the Lord entered into a dark experience when all should have been light. Doubt began to enter into her experience because her prayers were not answered. It was doubt that brought doubt into her spirit. When you doubt one thing you doubt everything.

This Christian lady decided to try any and every method of prayer to receive answers. She tried keeping quiet before the Lord, to see if maybe she was speaking too much and was not allowing the Lord time to speak to her inner being. Was it impatience that was standing in the way of answers? Instead of answers there were more questions, questions more than prayers began to arrange themselves in her mind. 'In quietness and confidence shall be your strength,' Isaiah 30:15. Yes she would believe that. This was tried day after day, month after month, but there was still no answer to the cry of her heart. Instead of her waiting on the Lord, and mounting up with wings of eagles, Isaiah 40:32, Susan found that her wings were moulting and there was degeneration rather than a new generation of power that comes through answered prayer. The words had seemed imprisoned within her mouth, and instead of the tongue of the learned she felt like a child learning the alphabet, using unfamiliar words and unable to get a parent to respond.

Opening her Bible she began to pray the word of God just like the Chinese and the Koreans do, quoting the promises of the Lord to the One who made the promise. God would surely become the echo of His own word. A response would come from the Responsible. Still heaven and earth seemed as a closed prison cell and her prayers as dry and dusty as a desert after a sand storm. Maybe she wasn't praying enough chapters. So the chapters were increased from one to two, three, four and more. Something from the Old and something from the New Testament should triumph. Why wouldn't God honour His word? The answer to her prayer still seemed far removed, as far as the east is from the west.

Then she had an idea: why not keep repeating the Lord's Prayer, and let the Father interpret His daughter's needs. This seemed like a good idea. Off she went with Bible, glass of water and handkerchief to wipe away the sweat. The Lord's Prayer was repeated parrot fashion more than any parrot had every repeated anything. Different versions of the Lord's Prayer were tried, but they seemed to be weighed in the balance and found wanting.

Tired, sweating and worried Susan came out of prayer every time feeling worse than she had when she went into prayer. Praying the Lord's Prayer she felt was going to be the answer because these were the very words of Jesus Christ. Then different versions between Matthew's Gospel and the account in Luke were tried. One included the words 'the power and the glory' while the other version omitted these words of power and authority. All was to no avail. The only answer she received was the monotonous ticking of the clock by the bedside as if it was mocking her, and saying: Listen, I answer without you speaking to me!

Someone told her that if she repeated her prayers, wearing a crucifix, while allowing beads to pass through her fingers that would produce the desired results. In fact the person who suggested it swore by it as they finished the sentence with a swear word. This was a foolproof way of getting answers to prayer. That problem would disappear as if it had never existed. It would be erased, never to be remembered. Susan, at the end of her tether, was prepared to try anything to receive an answer to her prayers. She tried repeating prayers as beads passed through her fingers, followed by a few hail Marys! —but alas the only beads had been beads of sweat! This was no solace to her soul. She was going around in ever decreasing circles. Her spirit seemed to be getting smaller and smaller, while the fear and the doubt, the problem unresolved, was growing out of all proportion. The feeling entered her that made her as small as the beads that had been ceremoniously passed through her tender fingers. Susan felt bound hands and feet as the beads were attached together by links of a chain to one another. As they moved not from the chain, so no answer was received.

Visiting the local Christian bookshop, she

saw books that had lovely colourful covers with the title 'Fasting and Prayer'; 'Prayer without Fasting', and 'Fasting with Prayer'. 'Ah,' she thought, as she saw the multicoloured books 'These might have the answer to my deep need.' They were purchased, and the assistant informed her 'We don't sell many of that sort of book nowadays. Most people like to buy exciting books about miracles with signs and wonders, particularly if they are told they can happen in the first month of conversion.' That was a surprise to Susan, as she left the shop clutching the new volumes, and stumbling as she tried to read part of the Introduction of one of them, as she passed over the lip of the doorstep.

Many days were spent reading about prayer and fasting. The author dealt with it from many angles, and seemed to assure every reader that by following what was suggested, rather like following the directions on a medicine bottle, when applied, gently rubbed in during prayer, the need would be met, the prayer would be answered and the soul would be settled. Fasting speaks louder than words, and that is why it is so needful, was the advice given.

With great aplomb, the book was not just tasted but swallowed from cover to cover, devoured as a hungry lion that had not eaten for days. The reading of the blurb on back and front would have been fully followed if this would have met her deep need. Whatever the penman suggested she would do. Days of prayer followed, and then more weak days of prayer and fasting as Susan grew weak with weariness. She felt like one in a great battle where you get so weak and wet through with weariness that the weapon cleaves to your hand. This went on for six months of toil, toil and more toil. It was fully understood through this experience what the Lord meant when He told Adam that he would have to toil in the sweat of his brow. It felt as if this Eve had become a tiller of the soil.

'That certainly didn't work,' muttered Susan, and there was the expectation that the Lord would hear that remark rather than her prayers. Maybe if she changed her position in prayer that might help. 'I will make myself more humble by kneeling on the bare floor, and then laying my face on the floor,' thought the woman. This was tried until the result was housemaid's knee and a sore stomach. Being unable to breathe properly, she felt that she was choking. Every posture a contortionist might try was tried but she was not bettered by it, but like the woman with the issue of blood she began to feel worse, Mark 5:26. Here was a woman with a will of steel, but even that steel was being bent. 'What a wretch I am,' she thought, 'nothing seems to work for me, maybe I should just stop praying, and leave the world to get on with its own way of doing things.' This conclusion of a suffering saint was no answer, but provided many a question. It seemed as if she knew more and more about less and less.

Self doubt began to multiply like weeds after the rain. Was it her faith that was lacking? Time and again different methods had been tried, but the ladder always seemed too short, the target never struck, the prayer never answered. Had God gone on holiday (modern translation) as Elijah had said of the god of the prophets of Baal in 1 Kings 18:27? Susan didn't even know if God took holidays or not. The one thing she did know was that when and where she had prayed there had been no answer to her problem. All that had happened was that the problem wound itself around her more tightly the more she prayed. Who would deliver her from this body of death, this ongoing relentless burden that was growing by the day until it would out-grow the day, and leave her bleeding with frustration?

A leaflet was given to her announcing that Terry and Margaret Atkinson were coming to minister in her church. Hope began to spring. 'I wonder if Margaret could tell me how to get answers to my prayers,' she thought. Susan attended the meeting more out of duty than faith, to receive an answer to what was troubling her.

Susan responded to the appeal, and, as she walked forward in doom and gloom, a light shone from the face of Margaret as God began to sermonise her heart. Here were two daughters of Eve and Sarah coming together — one representing creation, the other faith.

As Margaret was waiting to receive Susan, God began to say to Margaret, "Tell her to try 'liquid prayers.'" This happened a split second before Susan came face to face with her. Susan began to explain the patterns she had used to receive answers to prayer, but had received none, and was wondering if it was worth continuing to pray. Even before the seeker had said a word, Margaret knew what she was going to say. The answer was within her spirit.

'The Lord says,' Margaret said, 'Try liquid prayers.' 'I have never heard that term before,' Susan said, 'I don't know what you mean, please explain it to me.' They both sat down together as daughters born into the same family with the same Father.

'There are prayers and prayers,' explained Margaret. 'All your prayers have been as dry as a dusty well. You have tried many methods of prayer, but you have never let your tears do the praying.'

Susan, gasped, as if she had been hit by some invisible dart. What was said went straight to her heart. 'You mean to say,' she gasped, then continued, 'I have never really wept in my times of prayer? My heart has never been broken into pieces?'

'That is right,' Margaret assured her. 'When small boats sail they need water, and sometimes there needs to be tears in our prayers so that the answers can come sailing right to where we are. The seeds you are trying to sow need to be planted, but they will never grow unless they are watered. Each plant requires rain, and in your case, your prayers need to be baptized in tears. Not to be sprinkled, but to be baptized,' again Margaret assured her. 'Those tears mirror your heart, and tell God more than words how you really feel. As you let your tears flow, Jesus will come with the answers walking on those tears as He walked on the water. Those tears are useful to the Potter of the soul, for He can use them to form you into the clay vessel of His choice and unto His honour. Tears speak with a voice of their own that is beyond human intellect or inspiration.' Margaret reminded Susan, 'Poets of old used to mix their tears with their paints, and the painting was so glorious with the tears added. These tears put punch into their paintings. The artist expected to see others cry when they saw the results of their tears mixed with paint, wedded together on a palate, and then added to the canvas with a fine brush. Dry prayers never touch the heart of God, but when we wet them with our tears we lustre them with love.' Susan breathed a sight of relief. She had been told a way of escape from her prison of frustration.

A few months passed. Susan came rushing to where Margaret was and, flinging her arms around her she cried, 'It works! It works! What you told me about liquid tears brings results, because I asked God to move me as I prayed, He did, and I began to pray liquid prayers, and the answer came that met my need. I gave my tears but He gave His heart.'

The Jewish nation used to keep their tears in a bottle when they were grief stricken, Psalm 56:8, and those tears were kept as a memorial of their suffering. The tears reminded them of the hardship of suffering. Tears that are shed at the feet of Jesus are not wasted; they do not flow away, but can be turned into pearls as we receive answers to prayer.

The tears of Jesus have been saved for us in John 11:35, kept in a promise in a word from the Lord to remind us of His suffering and what unbelief does to the heart of God. They are there so that we not only quote the text but weep tears as Jesus did.

15

REJUVENATED
IN RETIREMENT

If success is measured in numbers and a large church building, then Sam was certainly successful. What had been a normal Pentecostal Church with a membership of 100, Sam, by the grace of God, had seen grow into hundreds. Flags were positioned around the auditorium to remind everyone of the nations that needed reaching with the gospel of Jesus Christ. The flags expressed Sam's missionary vision. He had seen the original church split, and then grow into a strong congregation. The church had moved from different premises, and the one they now occupied had been converted into a church. He had been involved in the planning, motivating, and finalising of all the things relative to the church of which he was the senior minister.

Sam was more than the normal minister; the marks of an apostle of the church of Jesus Christ were seen in his life of prayer, devotion and passion. Many churches came into existence because of his passion and vision for the lost. If there was a need, it was Sam who would arrive at the doorstep with a gift of money and food that was required. He was a church planter, an inspirer of others, the one to turn to in a time of need. He spent hours, days and months travelling the length and breadth of England. Early mornings and late nights were part of his daily routine.

Sam had spent a period of time in Australia, and after travelling to many countries had a worldwide knowledge of the church of Jesus Christ. His past experiences had been a training ground for the future, although at the time of his conversation with Margaret Atkinson, Sam did not fully understand how God had been using the past as an engraving tool. He was not the finished article, but what he lacked in diplomacy in dealing with others he made up for with his white hot zeal and love for Jesus Christ.

To be in his presence was a benediction. He inspired young and old, strong and frail. After he had spoken to you, there was the feeling in your heart that you could and would be a world conqueror. He had the ability to speak life into lifeless forms. The same God who raised Jesus from the dead was at work here. Young and old used to hang onto his every word. The feeling was that word spoken, or the advice given, sometimes as a father, at other times as a friend, could be trusted through thick and thin, and would take you through hell and high water. The strength of the man was that he did not just give good advice, but gave it out of a thoughtful heart, and out of the abundance of his large experience.

Sam never asked anyone to do what he himself was not prepared to do. If you were to go down into a pit, he was the one who would hold the rope or the ladder until you descended, he would not be happy until you ascended. At the bottom of the pit you would find Sam sitting next to you. Any topic from birth to death, divorce or marriage he had something to say about. This man was an encyclopaedia on physical and eternal life.

Sam was of the old school. There was little counselling, and if there was any at all it was short and to the point. Time wasters received 'short shrift'. He believed that if God said it, that settled it if you believed it. He did not hang around when praying, but went straight to the point, and after prayer he believed that the Lord had answered, and he acted on that knowledge. Sam believed in casting mountains into the sea and the sea into mountains!

During a pastoral consultation with Sam, many hurts were healed and many broken hearts found the pieces that had been shattered. The methods he used worked time and time again. Those coming into his presence with sad faces usually departed with beams of glory shining from them. Here was a bishop who could take sheep and lead them into greener pastures.

Sam had a glory that few men possessed. There was nothing dull about him or hypocritical. He shunned sham! There were times when I had been to him for counselling and came out of his study refreshed. He believed that you should attempt great things for God, and expect great things from God. He made mistakes, but who looks at the weeds while the flowers are revealing their colours? If you had a flower in you, he would give it a chance to grow and bloom. Sam's advice if you mentioned his faults was 'Burn my weeds, cultivate my flowers.'

It was a Wednesday morning, dull and grey as Manchester, England can be at this time of the year. The telephone rang, (it sounded like the noise of the ambulance or fire engine on a mercy dash with its tone subdued), Margaret answered it in her usual gentle manner, and always calling everybody 'love'. This immediately removed any hostility. Frayed nerve ends were healed in the quietness of the answering voice as Margaret spoke to those in need, or even those who were time wasters wanting to sell what she already possessed. Even those making 'cold calls' were witnessed to as the conversation was turned to Jesus Christ and what He could do for the caller. Usually, when Margaret thrust the topic of salvation on the caller, there was an embarrassing silence for a few minutes. The hunter had been hunted and caught!

It was Sam on the telephone asking for Terry. He used to come straight to the point, 'Is he in?' 'No, he is not here at the moment, but he will be in later,' was Margaret's calm and collected reply. This was followed by disappointment entering into the caller's voice. Before Sam rang off he said to Margaret, 'I would like to pray for you?' Margaret's reply took him by surprise. 'No,' she said 'I will pray for you.' Margaret began to pray for Sam, and as she prayed the windows of heaven opened and the flood began to rise in her spirit. Margaret was praying the blessing of Jacob, Isaac and Abraham upon this man of God. The Spirit of the Lord came upon His handmaiden, and inspiration began to flow in many directions towards Sam.

Margaret had been seeking the Lord in prayer, and Sam was the person that God had brought before her. The Lord had something to say to Sam, and He wanted the prophetess to prophesy to Sam what the Lord wanted him to know. The words Margaret said were like honey and healing to the spirit of Sam. If Sam had chosen the words himself they could not have been better chosen to meet his need. These were golden apples in silver pictures.

Margaret knew that Sam had resigned from his church. He had come to the conclusion that he did not want to hang on to the church too long, and empty it as he had seen many of his friends do. There was no glory or accomplishment in staying too long. Sam had spent years training young people, and a Leadership Team was in place, so he felt it was time to resign, and to let a younger man, whom he had trained, become the leader of the church. He spent much time praying and pondering. This was a big decision, and the implications were far greater than Sam had ever conceived.

It was his world that he was surrendering, seemingly without a fight. He was going out like a zephyr, when it should have been like a tornado! There was no ointment that would heal what he was feeling. He knew bad decisions lead to bad feelings.

Suddenly the life of Sam was so empty. He had come to a full stop. It was not just a stop but a free fall into oblivion. He had been like one rushing along as a river, and suddenly the flow had been stopped, as it was when the Lord cut off the River Jordan. There was a mid life crisis, and yet he was at the latter end of life! He had wanted to get away from it all but in his wildest moments he never thought it would be like this. He was verging on depression.

Where was the God of the past? Some had thought it had been glamorous, but it had had its difficult moments. Where were the crowds now? There was no adulation in retirement. The church he had pastored for so many years had given the customary gifts, had said their words of appreciation, but it all seemed so empty, as empty as a box without a gift.

Had he made a mistake? Was this the worst moment of his life? This was worse than being put up to a wall and being shot for desertion. He did not deserve this. He deserved better things after serving the Lord for so many years. It was like going from the firing line into the medical corps.

He began to realise, if he had not realised it before, that you are not in the kingdom by merit but by grace alone. God buried His workmen, but even when good men are buried, they begin to build a foundation from below. He must throw himself into the Everlasting Arms and let grace do its healing work. The conviction gripped his heart that he had nowhere else to go, and no one else to turn to. Would there never be a way out of this dark wood?

Sam's wife Sylvia was awakened in the night. Sam was crying by the side of his bed. He was asking 'Why, Lord, why Lord, why me Lord? Oh, Lord if only I had known, I would have done it differently.' Sam rarely cried, and when he did you knew they were not crocodile tears, but real tears from the hurt of the heart. Between the sobs Sylvia could hear him praying, 'Lord, will you open up some other way, another door. Have you finished with your servant? Has my life now come to this end which is hell on earth?' An alphabet of questions were pouring from his spirit as he prayed, each word bathed in tears. His face looked as if it was in a storm as the tears ran down to his chin and onto the floor to stain it with grief.

He would swing between emotions as a child on a swing; one moment he was happy, the next he was snappy. There was no 'middle ground' on which he stood. High was high and low was low, so low. In his spirit he had made his home with the snails and worms! He felt that he was no man only a worm.

Sam had worked faithfully for the Lord but that one decision altered everything. It had drawn the curtain on a beautiful life, so he thought. God had greater ideas for him, and those ideas were being passed on to a servant of the Lord, Margaret Atkinson, who received what the Lord had to say with an open heart, and simply said, 'Lord, speak for your servant is listening.' Margaret listened, and heard the voice of the Lord. Not clamouring for a 'word' for herself, but for another with a greater need. This was the time of the grief of Rachel who would not be comforted, because her children had been removed, Matthew 2:18. She would have to contact Sam, and she needed the courage to pass on what the Lord had told her.

There were times when Margaret would

telephone a minister or his wife, and reveal what the Lord had said to her. These words were like jewels. It was at moments like this that rainbows appeared in dark skies, and the time of mourning was replaced by a song of joy. Many times when it seemed that dark despair had come to sit on the throne, that despair was toppled by a word from Margaret. The powers of darkness and discouragement were overthrown because of one word from the Lord; one word of command and all was under command. Margaret was sent into the fore of the battle as one bearing good news from afar.

That which had been received in the quiet place must be made known from the housetops. This would take obedience and boldness on Margaret's part, because she felt that Sam was difficult to speak to, although others found him friendly and approachable. The timidity of Margaret's childhood days must be forgotten. How would she approach the subject of Sam's retirement? Margaret prayed that God would provide an opening for her to speak, to give her a platform into another's life.

It was at this moment that the telephone rang. Margaret was already speaking to Sam. She must speak to the open ear as he could do nothing else but listen. After a brief conversation as to her health and other matters, Margaret jumped in, both feet first. It was now or never, better now than never! 'I have something from the Lord to say to you, Sam,' Margaret said. 'The Lord has told me that your best years are yet to come. There is a far greater ministry ahead of you than you have ever dreamed was possible.' There was a hesitation, and she could hear in the silence that what was being said could not be fully understood or appreciated. Margaret felt that as she had commenced the conversation she must complete it. The truth the whole truth and nothing but the truth must be stated.

Speaking to Sam under the anointing of the Holy Spirit was easy, but as the words came from Margaret's lips she heard a sharp intake of breath, as if Sam could not believe what Margaret was saying. God had revealed to her that his best years were yet to be. The past had only been a shadow of the influence that he would exert now that he had retired. The shock to Sam was indescribable, because he felt like a beggar being told that he was going to be a prince. These words were better in his ears than a prisoner given a pardon and set free. There was far more for him in the future than there had ever been in the past. The past was history but this was spirituality with wings on. Margaret told Sam that he would travel the world, going from country to country as an ambassador of Jesus Christ. He would influence far more people than he had ever influenced in his church life. Sam would touch millions of lives through his abilities and teaching. He would be a wise shepherd to many countries in the world. God had other sheep that were not of Sam's old fold. This was something sparkling and new. No plan was to be formulated because God would piece his future together like two hands being together to make one grasp. As Margaret began to unpeel that wrapped up in a skin, she distinctly heard a laugh. It was the sort of laugh that Sarai had given when being told by an angel that in her old age she would conceive and have a child, Genesis 18:12–15.

The silence of that moment of doubt was broken by the voice of Sam; his voice seemed to be much further away than it had been before, as if he was standing back and away from this prophecy. 'That will be a fine thing!' he said. 'If God is going to do that He hasn't told me. It will be wonderful if it happens.' In Margaret's mind the old proverb seemed to be reversed. 'He who laughs longest laughs last.' The full stop to the promise of the Lord was a laugh. Margaret placed the telephone back on to the receiver as Sam said goodbye to her, filled with wonder and concern about what he had heard.

Some years later I heard Sam testifying how God had met his need when he was disturbed. Other people besides Margaret confirmed what God was going to do. Sam is now a representative of a church fellowship, and as a coordinator travels from one country to another. Sam's advice is like that of Ahithophel who used to give King David and Absalom advice, 2 Samuel 15, 16 and 17. He is busier than ever. He never seems to have time for himself. The God that neither slumbers nor sleeps brought him out of the deep sleep of retirement into a new area that he felt would never have been possible. He was reminded, as we all are, that with God nothing is impossible.

16

THE SHATTERED IMAGE

Alan was as tall as he was handsome. He knew that he was good looking, and would spend many hours before a mirror. In himself he thought he resembled a Greek god. The sad thing was that he measured beauty by facial expressions and how he felt. In fact Alan felt that he was so handsome, the image in the mirror should step out of the glass and become his twin, and then he would be twice as handsome! The Greek gods were his measure of beauty; Zeus, Apolion, Hermes, Poseidon were his idols. He desired to be like them in physique and manner of living. 'Built for the kill', he felt any female could be influenced and fall under his charm.

There was a snake nature lurking beneath his human nature. Whenever he preached, Alan spent as much time preparing himself as he spent preparing his message for the people he pastored. Time that should have been spent in prayer and on his knees was spent on his face! No hair was out of place, no part of his face was missed as he applied soothing cream. There was a glow on his face, but it was not a holy glow, it was self administered and applied by pride of place, race and face. The suit was neatly pressed, the eyebrows plucked, the face clean; every bead of sweat was followed by a lotion that hid the signs of ageing.

These hands had never washed dishes. Every line of age that appeared was frowned upon. If he had been a miracle worker, the marks of ageing would have been banished to where they came from. Alan put as much work as a labourer on a building site in managing his beauty. He felt that what had been given at birth by God should be maintained frequently, in fact as often as he could. His wife wondered if he would wear the mirror out as he constantly stood before it, parading his gifts as one in a fashion show.

God had granted him a miracle, and it was a fact that he was an 'oil painting'. When the Eternal was giving out good looks, Alan certainly was not last or lost in the queue. To those who knew him, he was the Greek youth Adonis gazing into the waters, in love with himself. He was a perfect description of the Greek word 'grace', 'fullness of form' in every department. God had given to him in natural birth that which was pressed down, shaken together and running over. He felt he could have been a male model! Anyone with a camera would be sure to want to take his photograph. Here was royalty in rags, the rags of his own thinking. He would grace a strip of film or fashion show where beauty that is only skin deep or applied from a toning bottle or cream would suffice. Maybe he should have been a film star, and if not, he felt that he was Hollywood!

Alan's main concern when he ministered was not how he preached or what he said, the content of the message did not matter; it was how he appeared before the congregation. His looks were his passport to acceptance. Without his beauty of form no one would accept him. That is why Alan needed to keep working on what had been given to him. What he was slept, ate, walked and talked with him all day long, and his good looks were his paradise of Eden. If he felt discouraged, he gazed in the mirror instead of 'looking unto Jesus the author and finisher of our faith,' Hebrews 12:2.

Alan never liked it when people prayed that the preacher might be hidden behind the cross. That would lessen his appeal, would turn a beautiful swan intro an ugly duckling. Seeing him was better than seeing the sun set or the moon rise surrounding by twinkling stars, or so he thought. His wife Daisy had married him 'for better or worse', and Alan thought he was the 'better' part of this marriage. Daisy had bettered herself by marrying him.

Daisy called Margaret and said, 'Margaret can

you seek the Lord for my husband, and ask the Lord to give you something to say to him? If you receive any word from the Lord, will you pass it on?' Daisy was desperate, because she knew the vanity of her partner in life. Living with him was like living in a beauty parlour. She didn't think he had ever fallen in love with her; he was too much in love with himself. He was a self-made man and was madly in love with his creator. It seemed to her as if he was a doctor of beauty. As a child he had sketched drawings of himself while other boys played football! While they played with their miniature railway, he was busy looking for new lotions. Their marriage was under a strain, and she wanted the Lord to help where she could only cry. It was after Margaret had received something from the Lord that the true facts about Alan became known. The clandestine became clear.

Margaret was always ready, willing and able to seek the Lord, for in seeking the Almighty, He always gave her from His might, revealing things as they actually were, not as people thought they were. The Lord never fitted into man's conception or misconception. Margaret's happiest moments were when she knelt at the cross, seeking the Lord for others in distress. He was healing for the helpless. Without any knowledge of the couples' affairs, Margaret went to ask God about the matter. She never did leave the Lord's presence without the Bread of Life. When you are in touch with

Jehovah, He is never far from you. If you seek advice, then it is readily given and received with thanks.

Sometimes Margaret would receive a word of encouragement for another. On other occasions it would be a word of rebuke, or a word of exhortation. It would always be a whisper in her ear from the Lord that would make the matter right. Sometimes she felt that her voice was the one crying in a wilderness. Although that which she received from the Lord was in the stillness of quietness it was always a sure word that would produce a sure foundation. When the Almighty speaks He never leaves you in 'no man's land' nor is He ever indecisive. That spoken is clearer than a cuckoo call in the spring of the year or the dawn of the day.

Margaret began to pray that God would reveal the secrets of this man's life. God knows the heart, and the source of our desires, the thoughts of the heart are weighed in the balances. As she prayed, she saw Alan standing erect as a soldier of the Queen of England on parade wearing a multi-coloured uniform straightening his tie. He was dressed as if he was going on parade on the occasion of the Queen's Birthday Celebration. He was better attired than a tailor's dummy. It was as if he had been called into the presence of the Queen by 'Royal Command'. In another form of creation he would have been a peacock, preened and primed, better than 'ship shape and Bristol fashion'. God had granted Alan good looks that should be pampered as much as possible. What Alan omitted to think or recognise is that the One who gives with the right hand can take away with the left. Looks are only for this life and have no part or lot in eternal life. Age and mortality would deny his affair with himself. The battle would be fought to the last man, if it meant establishing his good looks. Alan did not realise that a losing battle was being fought, looks only last as long as there is something to see. Vanity was the order of the day, and in 'Pilgrim's Progress' Alan would have frequented 'Vanity Fair', to buy and sell, to smell the perfumes and see the physical forms that he found so attractive. He felt that a part in 'Sleeping Beauty' should have been his, and he could fulfil the role admirably. What he did not understand was that the Almighty viewed such vanity as being like the 'wicked witch' who fed 'Snow White' a poisoned apple. The nature of wickedness had been fed into his spirit.

Actions are louder than good looks! How we act tells what we are, where we are, and where we are going. Life is not a ball, and we are not handsome princes or princesses travelling to it. We will have to face the ugly, stunted, twisted and torn. The real grace that Alan lacked was to see beauty in that which was ugly, seeing a frog turned into a beautiful Prince Charming. There is an outward beauty, and there is that which is within being changed from one stage of glory to another. The outward man seen in Alan perishes, and we must minister to that lasting longer than earth's verities. The outward man will grow old as we grow old, but that which is in God is eternal. We require that which does not grow old as we grow old, but has integral everlasting beauty

God would take Alan into His School of Learning then he would understand that it is not outward show or measure that commends us to God, but the hidden man of the heart. It is the nature of Jesus Christ developed in us, so that through us the beauty of Jesus might be seen. John records that Jesus went about doing 'good', Acts 10:38, and the same word is used to describe in John 10 the 'good' shepherd. It means 'making things beautiful'. When we seek to beautify what we have, the outward is what we work on, but when God performs a work it is from the inside. The beauty of the Lord our God that is upon us, (Psalm 90:17) is a meek spirit, gentleness, faithfulness, longsuffering, patience. These are the inner fruit of the heart that the Lord is looking for. It is of eternal quality that makes us what we are in the presence of the Lord who sees within the thin veil of skin that surrounds us.

Alan gazed longingly at the mirror as if that mirror was his god, (the image reflected in the mirror was), and he was praying to it to reveal his looks in greater detail. He felt he was falling in love with love — love of self. In his mind he would mutter 'Mirror, mirror on the wall, who is the fairest of us all, and why am I?'

Alan felt that the Greek gods continued in him. There was love here, but it was love for himself that needed to be channelled to help others. The beauty of one remains with one's own features, but when released by faith the beauty of Jesus Christ goes to whosoever will believe. When Alan sang 'Let the beauty of Jesus be seen in me', he meant something quite different to what the hymn suggests. A small nose, a well shaped mouth, lovely cheek bones, ears like velvet, hands that were soft and small; these were part of this man's treasure trove. He had no need to open his trinket box; he just gazed in the mirror with an expression of adoration. He was his own creator and he adored that creator. What had he to do with photographs or a scrapbook while he could stand before the mirror as the fairest thing on God's earth? Alan didn't require a scenic or breathtaking view; he simply went and stood by the mirror.

As Alan turned from the mirror strong and true, what he was suddenly turned into clay. The man suddenly became a clay man with many markings on his features. Margaret prayed on, and as she prayed a small hammer came out of the heavens and hit Alan on the crown of his head. There was a surprise in her spirit because the hammer, so small, wrought a lot of damage on the image that was being presented. The man's head was treated as if it was a nail, and the hammer came with full force to the head of the nail. There were no repeated blows as when a nail is being knocked into a short piece of wood. Just one blow from the hammer did the damage. Margaret knew that the word of God is described as a hammer, Jeremiah 23:29. It was a small hammer but it had unmeasured power.

What Margaret saw next made her sad. What was young and beautiful, dressed in full fashion, suddenly turned into white clay. Lines began to travel all over that youthful face making it so ugly. The lines had carved the image into many pieces. Youth had suddenly aged before her eyes. It was too much for her mind to accept. No blood ran from those wounds to the face. The lacerations yielded no fluid. It looked like cracked clay in the bed of a river that had dried up. It had the appearance of a bar of toffee being struck with a toffee hammer, and the pieces breaking into large and small. There was no shape about the face; it was just a gathering of crooked lines, shattered as a broken vessel, never to be restored to its former glory. The handsome had lost its glory; the face which represents the personality was just as other men.

As Margaret gasped and then waited with bated breath; the whole image of a man was reduced to a small pile of dust, so small that a duster could have wiped it away. You could have taken the dust, run your finger through it and left an uncertain message. The Lord said to Margaret, 'Tell Alan that I am going to remake him from the dust, he will be a phoenix, rising out of the ashes. I will be a Father to him and he shall be a son to Me. Together we can make it tall and strong without the added human beauty. The human beauty has no 'part or lot' in this matter.

In the past if a gnat touched his face, or a spot mark appeared, Alan would have reached into his medicine chest, and would have added cream to the mark. There was nothing that would cover this scarred face reduced to dust. Nothing would ever bring it back to its vain repetition. Virgin beauty had been destroyed, and Alan felt as sad as a child robbed of an ice cream! Alan had the means to cover up anything distasteful or any appearance other than what he determined would be. He had the means to sustain and create beauty. Beauty to him was not a thing of the past, it was given to last.

Alan went from being so beautiful into what was a pile of white clay, as fine as salt. What had been strong, desirable and manly was turned into measured dust. It looked like white sand taken from a desert where nothing will ever grow unless it rains. Where now was all his beauty and good thoughts of himself? All had been reduced to a pile of dust. Yet, dust that the Lord could use.

God's voice interrupted the vision, and God said, 'Tell Alan, I am going to break him into that which is as small as powder particles, and from the pile of powder clay I am going to make a new man. The beauty that I give will be of the heart, inward and not outward, for eternity and not for time. That given by Me will not grow old as beauty grows old. It will not degenerate in a human form. From that small, ugly measure I will create My beauty, for My tools are not carnal. It will be as fresh in the morning as in the evening, and as My nature it will not fail or falter. It will always be as I intended it to be. This man will be God's man, and over a period of time, I am going to smash that delusive image Alan has of himself, and will transform him into the image of Jesus Christ.

'The demon of self worship will be destroyed. From that pile of clay there will be a new beauty that is more than skin deep. It will be the beauty of heaven, and will last as long as eternal life. The man before the mirror will not want to adjust it to suit his vision of himself or have to preen this new beauty. It will be something that will develop without his assistance. What I the Lord reduced to ashes will be rebuilt into the glory, honour, majesty and dominion of the new birth. What Jehovah did with the seed of Abraham, likened unto the sand by the seashore, He will do with the remaining particles of this life.'

When Margaret heard and saw that, she felt

dismayed because Alan would have to be told what God had revealed. When it was repeated it would be as strong as the hammer she saw coming from the sky. Daisy would have to be contacted and the message would be passed on. Margaret played her part as an echo of His voice in repeating to Daisy what was not as a gospel of good news, but the sad news of a man's demise, because the Lord will have no other gods before Him.

17

THE BOWL AND
THE TOWEL

The church, in the north of England, was a pioneer work, and had only been in existence for a few months. There is usually an air of anticipation when visiting a new church; the atmosphere has not been polluted by arguments or rivalry, the order of service is not so rigid, and the new people have the freedom of revival in their spirit. Like a new born baby it has so much to offer.

Margaret was taken to the church by her daughter, Lindsay. As they arrived, many had gathered for this weekend of praise and worship. Margaret, as was her custom, sat near the back of the church. From this position she could see the congregation with a clear eye. The people sat in multi-coloured dresses, from every walk of life. There was a 'buzz' about the place, and the people had gathered expecting God to meet the needs of the heart through the heart and hands of Jesus

Christ who had suffered on a cross. They had come with one purpose, and that was to worship the living God. After spending much of the week surrounded by dead idols it was a breath of spring air to be in the presence of the Lord, to feel as free as the wind blowing on the hills around this city.

The leader of the church was a lady who was skilled in guiding the people of God in worship. Desiree, the lady pastor, stood out as she led the worship in a forthright manner, with her black hair adding to her beauty. Here was a woman with zeal, and a mission. Desiree was not building her future on hurts but on hope, and in this service hope was being set free for all to partake and enjoy what the Almighty had for them. In Desiree we were witnessing a 'purpose driven life'. It does happen now and again that it seems as if the Eternal reserves His best for the prodigal returning home to put shoes on the feet, a garment on the back and an anointed smile on the face. All these qualities were in evidence. There was the constant reassurance to any who were coming to the Lord or were visiting this assembly for the first time. Here in the Lancashire city was a little bit of heaven on earth. How good it was to retire from the world and those around! It was here that the saints could be 'perfected' — brought back into synchronisation. Hurts would be healed as lives were challenged through the preaching of the word. Above and beyond all other conversation, one voice was to be heard, acknowledged and obeyed, and that was the voice of the Spirit of God. What He had to say became as precious as an only child.

As Margaret began to meditate, she was very conscious of the presence of the Holy Spirit. In her spirit she was not looking at a congregation of different colours, she was gazing at one heart, seeing one life depicted before her. God began to reveal the needs of the lady Pastor, Desiree.

To others she appeared confident, loving and gracious. The boldness of the Acts of the Apostles was upon her as she was immersed in the Holy Spirit. What the burdens of her heart were nobody knew but God. Only God can measure and weigh a burden. What is a dark leaden night is broken up by the appearance of the dawn. What was heavy to Desiree was light to God. When He turns that heavy and difficult thing into a feather, He even sends the wing that the feather flies through the air with to carry to our destination, having the wings of the eagle. The Almighty knows all things; He has known them, does know them and will know them. As Margaret worshipped in this meeting, the Lord, who knows and sees everything, was speaking His words into her heart.

God was giving good measure, pressed down, shaken together and running over. The wise men came to offer gifts most rare to Jesus, (Matthew

2:11) but God was offering Margaret gifts and insight that were also rare. Heaven opened up before her, and as only God can, He began to relate to Margaret the needs of this lady leader of the people of God.

Margaret was watching a video recording, in her spirit, of what the Lord wanted to communicate to the woman Pastor. Outwardly everything looked happy and complete, but inwardly there were things that Desiree needed help with. The work had been tough, the way long. The reward seemed sparse. Each step at this moment was a difficult one. Even the downhill was uphill all the way. The bends she had to go around were making her dizzy, but she had to recognise every happening as part of the potter's spinning wheel. Desiree simply accepted that if you walked around a thing long enough the walls would fall down as they did when Israel marched around the walls of Jericho, Joshua 6:20. You have to walk around most things before you can walk through them. You must inspect them before you can tread them under foot.

Margaret could see Desiree walking barefoot over rough ground. Blood was oozing from her battered feet. The ground was so rough that it cut into her feet, and she required mountaineer's shoes. It would have been easier to walk over a bed of nails or to walk through coals of fire and expect not to be hurt. Although the way was weary, there was a look of determination on Desiree's face.

Something of the flint nature had been given to her. She was prepared to take something even from weariness, make a good pair of shoes out of a weary, wet day, and walk on in the sunshine of God's grace. The journey seemed uphill all the way. There were no resting places, no arbour, no wooden benches placed alongside the hard road. The pathway was borrowed from the journeys of the children of Israel as they wandered for forty years, when they could have entered the Promised Land after a few months' marching through the wilderness. It should have been as the ascent of a flying bird, but Desiree was walking, not flying! The further she ascended, the steeper it seemed to be, yet it was not a mountain that Desiree was walking, but a flat road that was so difficult. When you are pained in your feet you feel every cobble, pebble and rise. There are those things that jar your spirit. When that sort of pain gets into your heart then you require the Great Physician to heal you. It was so difficult that every tread increased the burden. It was a long, hard way with no end in sight. The more she walked, the longer the road appeared. It was a long pathway that might lead to a little cottage.

There was a look of determination on Desiree's face. If she had been going through hell, she would have walked right through it. Although the road was rough, it did not dissuade her or make her look back. This woman was no wife of Lot, who looking back was turned into a pillar of salt, Genesis 19:26. There was more ground to be gained. Although a willing servant, life had taken its toll out of this spirited life. The heart of Desiree was larger than the road being walked. There were larger things in her spirit than she was walking on. That largeness of heart could take her to the moon if the Lord required it! From that large heart came the large steps that would ultimately take her to the goal.

It was not the slowness or the quickness of the pace, nor the size of the steps, it was what was on the inside that would take her through and bring her to her goal. Desiree required a 'second wind', in the Holy Spirit that would take her on, along and up to where the eagles build their nests. That received in her heart was not leading or pushing her on, it was walking beside her in the person of Jesus Christ.

When it seemed as if there was no stopping Desiree, she suddenly sat down as one with all hope cut off. It was as if she had missed the last train. Feeling abandoned, depression and despair took her on one side, and there she stayed. This was the place where no fruit grew, not even a blade of grass appeared. These emotions can minister to your spirit if you let them, and you can become depressed. I do not know how long Desiree stayed there, but it was long enough for the Lord to hear her prayers. In desperation she began to pray to the God of her life. It was as if Hagar had been cast under the tree with Ishmael on her back, short of water and prepared to die, but when Hagar prayed, the Lord appeared with words of comfort, Genesis 21:17. It was not the will of God for her to sit and stay in discouragement and depression. The clouds which might have sent rain to wash her away parted, and a beam of glory began to shine upon this distraught figure.

At this moment when depression and discouragement seemed to hold Desiree in steel bars, the King of Glory appeared. I have often been to a cinema as a child and watched films about cowboys surrounded by Indians, and when all seems lost the cavalry appear! It wasn't as if Christ came near, He had been there all the time. It was just that His presence had not been recognised, emotions like a raging sea had appeared, and Jesus appeared to be asleep in the boat, Mark 4:38. In her spirit the words of the disciples echoed, 'Master, don't you care that we are perishing?' Jesus would not calm the troubled seas by saying 'Peace; be still!' He was to work in another way because He is a God of variety, and brings the winds out of His treasures, Jeremiah 10:13.

As Christ came near, He laid aside His outer robe. In one hand was a bowl and in the other a towel. Here was a Christ prepared to work 'with' the worker, but also 'on' the worker. Jesus was prepared to apply the salve where it was needed. If it is hurt feet, then He will attend to our walk. What He does will wake the walk, and put strength into our feet, feet that feel as if we have walked off the end of the world and into the arms of the Saviour. Margaret noticed that where Desiree stopped, there Jesus stopped also and met her need.

The hole you stumble in, there you will find the grace and the person of Jesus Christ. This King of Glory knelt before Desiree and began to bathe her cut, swollen hurting feet with the water from the bowl, and then wiped them with a towel. The strokes from the towel were so gentle. His touch was as soft and as fresh as hair blowing gently over the face. These strokes from the towel that He held were better than the pen strokes of any writer, or a physician's touch, for here was Christ redesigning a life with the strokes of a towel! Margaret realised how boys, when she was young, were transformed by the mother's towel and water with soap, but this was a miracle on another scale. It was more than just water and wiping of feet.

The Lord was bathing the feet of this worker, so that they could travel further and do more. The feet were healed in the hands of Christ. As the towel and water were applied, new life was entering into the feet. Margaret knew that, after prayer by Peter and John in Acts 3, the man at the Gate Beautiful received strength in his ankle bones and feet. That man became the first Pentecostal dancer!

The feet of Desiree had to function in the role they were created for. Talent is doing what you were created to do. The will of God is not a street reference map but a relationship with the Lord. Here were feet and heart that were in danger of losing out, of stopping short of where they should take her. This lady had a calling, a role to fulfil, and Jesus had come to help her to achieve. God wanted to take her out of that depression, hurt and pain, and so with a bowl and towel He began to wash it away. Margaret thought, 'What bare essentials the Master uses when He wants to encourage us.' There was nothing scientific about what He did. An old fashioned method brought new life to tired feet. Those feet would walk much further once they had been held in His hands. They were going to be directed again onto the path that Desiree had been called to walk. There was new life in the hands, the towel and the water that came out of the basin, flowing to be used in His hands, that ministered to her feet.

If only Christians would be as willing to be used as this towel, water and basin were in the hands of Jesus, the church would be a better place. It was not larger feet that Desiree required, what she already possessed needed rejuvenating. The implements Jesus brought with Him, in His wisdom, He saw them as His tools. Such ordinary implements in the hands of Jesus can build much and do whatever the occasion may require.

As the Lord of glory began to bathe the feet, Margaret could see that they were bruised, cut and bleeding. These feet had been trodden on. They had been through many a battle. They were bruised when they might have been blessed. Had someone repeatedly trodden on them, bruising and hurting until they were blue and blooded? They were scarred with care and stress. Those feet had travelled many miles on a seemingly never ending journey, but now they had come to the Great Physician of love. The hurt feet rested with the One whose feet had had nails put into them when He was nailed to a cross. To understand Desiree's need, He only had to look at His own feet. The pain He had suffered gave Him an understanding of the full measure of her pain.

As Jesus bathed Desiree's feet, words were spoken that would help her. The words spoken activated the water, and turned it into miraculous water. The towel was better than hygienic bandages applied to bleeding feet. The eyes of Jesus seemed to say: What they have done to your feet, they did to My heart. All you need to do now is to walk on and follow me. I will lift you over the larger stones, and the smaller ones will develop strong feet for your body. When you come to cross a river I will put some of these hurtful stones where you can walk on them over the river of chance or change. Jesus was going to give her the places that her feet stood on.

The voice that was near her feet was telling her to let go of the past. If Desiree would do this she could move into a new day that He had prepared. The past was in the hurting, paining, bleeding feet, and was holding her back. That voice and the words spoken could become as shoes to the feet of this one on a journey, a long journey from earth to heaven. Jesus reminded Desiree that He had called her out of darkness into light, and to walk in the light as He was in the light. This was to be the dawning of a new day, produced out of aching feet. Feet that felt as if they would drop off at the next step were strengthened to go on, for that was the nature of her calling.

When Margaret returned home to Manchester, she began to think on the things that God had said to her. These words and pictures became as jewels that should be like a necklace hung on Desiree's neck. Many times, after the event and after prayer and meditation, Margaret would contact the person for whom she had received something from the Lord. Margaret was a ready mediator of 'better things' and a messenger that carried good news from afar, described as cold water to a thirsty throat, Proverbs 25:25. Margaret believed in letting the word of the Lord percolate before it was passed on. As she waited on the Lord, it could be examined minutely and from every angle, so that nothing would be missed out. Margaret never wanted to strain at a gnat and swallow a camel!

That passed on must be what has been passed on to her.

Prayerfully, Margaret began to write a letter to Desiree to tell her what had been witnessed. Using the pen as an instrument, sweet words of comfort that acted as a cordial on the spirit of Desiree were put into the letter, which was sent to Margaret's daughter Lindsay, who willingly passed it on. God had done His part, Margaret had acted in obedience as a mediator, and the rest of the story was to be worked out in the life of Desiree.

18

A PROMISE IN THE NIGHT

Margaret had been ill for about six years, and life was an uphill battle. Yet when tenacity is welded to truth then triumph must be the natural outcome. There are many ways that the Lord will bring us through: some through the fire, some through the flood, through the valley, some adversity, but all ways lead through the blood of Christ. In it all we discover an Advocate, an Avenue to take us on to the Answer. The way of the just is sometimes as hard as the way of the unbeliever, but in the unbeliever it works more unbelief, while in the believer it works an eternal weight of glory, 2 Corinthians 4:17. It cannot be weighed or measured, it is that which cannot be compared to the glory of this world. One is like a feather in the wind (the glory of this world) while the other is as pure gold, as a solid measure of assurance.

Believing God, Margaret Atkinson saw a promise in every rock, stone and difficulty. There was always a vein of gold in the hard rock. The metal for chariot wheels was found in these hard times. The armour of the would be champion was in these pieces of grit. If it was there, then this was the reason for the rugged and the rigour. Even when it was dark, that darkness was arched in a rainbow of many colours, adding to the dimensions of her faith. There will always be those who through prayer help to turn night into day. They move in faith from the realm of reason to the realm and reign of faith and acceptance.

This was a dark night, and what was required was a burning flame of light borrowed from the bush that burned but was not consumed, that Moses saw (Exodus 3:2). It was there as a token of Israel's suffering and release by the Lord. There are times in suffering when the darkness is so black it can be almost cut with a knife. Yet, as you trust, diamond qualities are in these dark mines of suffering. The Welsh nation is famous for its singing and choirs, songs that were produced in the valleys of Wales. When you do not trust there is no parting of the dark night, only the emptiness and the gloom.

The Lord of all mercy must be merciful as the God of all grace must be gracious. The God of all hope produces hope. He brings a promise for us to use as a pillow to prop us up, a source of strength and delight in the darkest night.

Margaret knew in her spirit that the promise Giver was also the promise Keeper. He who had said it shall be so would see it through to the end. The first note of hope would sound, and then every note would echo until that musical score would come to the end, and she would find a new beginning as a melody sprang up in the heart of a sufferer.

These promises of the Lord are part of His eternal, internal and external nature. The infernal cannot worship the Eternal. The light of day could be blown out easier than one promise fail. The sky would need props of wood if the promises of the Almighty should fail, fade or frustrate, Hebrews 1:3. If one should fail, then like a display of dominoes, one falling or failing would cause the others to fall. He upholds all things by the word of His power, Colossians 1:16—just one word! Not one promise had failed, but sometimes God withholds the fulfilment until we are ready to use the answer for His glory.

In each promise the glory of Jehovah shines so brightly that, even on the darkest night and the farthest distance from God, the promises are still seen as a holy glow. In each promise there is still something to illuminate the pathway that leads to the throne. When it seems as if every part of a promise has failed, there is still enough in it to lighten your way and bring you into fulfilment.

That given by God might not yet have been fulfilled, and there can be a delay until the final day. The promises are large, 'pressed down, shaken together and running over.' We are only at the 'pressed down' stage, there is much more before us. The ink these promises are written with, the computer used to type them, might fade and fuse, but the promise goes on. One promise has a thousand lights for the many generations who have trusted the word of God. Each new generation rises up to take hold of that which has been doubted by the previous generation. Margaret had not only to know these things but believe them in her heart.

It had been a hard day, and as the night enfolded it was like a wet blanket thrown over her. She felt that whatever was happening to her must be dealt with. The darkness deepened until nothing could be discerned. It was impossible to see the right hand from the left. Everything merged into darkness.

The Giant Despair took her soul within his castle, and threw away the key. This was the night for tossing and turning, up and down, as if there was a storm in the bedroom that couldn't be seen for the darkness. The corners of the room seemed darker than the rest of that bedroom. The only respite would be thoughts of the coming day that would obliterate the suffering of yesterday. Margaret longed for the morning as the marooned man longs to sight a ship, and cups his ears to listen for the breakers on the shore or to catch a sound of an approaching rescue party. The deeper the suffering and struggle, the more the arms of love embraced her, and squeezed the darkness out of that space. She was being gradually drawn into light, light that was perfumed and handsome. What had been a wrestling ring now became a throne room because God's Presence was in this abode. Light that was a blaze of the noonday sun filled the dark night. God had kept His most brilliant light for the darkest of nights. The Presence was larger than the darkness, for the darkness 'comprehended it not,' John 1:5. That Presence would grant beauty for ashes and dancing for mourning, it would 'break the day' and all the sunshine that had been hidden behind the midnight clouds would be revealed.

God who rules everywhere rules other powers. The shade was replaced by the silver of His presence; the darkness did not deepen but diminished as if its dark night was over. Light was coming again as the returning Lord when we will be raptured, 1 Thessalonians 4:17. This light was like a victor returning from battle.

In her mind Margaret had seen the light of a new day creep silently yet beautifully over the hills and through the vales where she had been raised in Yorkshire, England. What had been natural and in the mind was becoming a spiritual reality as the

Lord moved into that bedroom, converting it into a throne room.

The Spirit of God began to move as if brooding over the waters, Genesis 1:2. Margaret began to feel the warmth of the love of God as the Spirit of God began to inspire her to reach for new heights. When the Spirit of God rests on you, there is the feeling of Samson's strength, David's kingship, Solomon's wisdom and Jeremiah's burning fire within the bones. Suddenly she was not what she had been. What had been struggle, strife and pain was smoothed away as if by a hidden Hand, smoothing the spirit as if smoothing the creases out of the bedclothes. God was in the place, it became Jehovah Shama — the Lord was there, everything must bow in His presence. Jacob had lacked the experience when he said, 'God was in this place and I knew it not,' Genesis 28:16. What had been an affront and in attack was turned into assurance, assurance that would sow many seeds and result in a great harvest of glory seen in human nature.

The Spirit of God began to impress words upon this handmaiden's spirit. They were strong, forceful and yet gentle words, words that could melt and mould in the same breath. These words came from a new vocabulary. Here she was listening to the voice of the Spirit. These words were like wine, and so deep that they could never be reached by a human hand, so sublime they went out of the human vocabulary, and entered into the tongues of angels. Those words were not in a stutter. There was no hesitating or groping for the next word or sentence. The Speaker was not out of His depth going into a realm unknown, beyond the curve of His mind. He had no need to quote others for others quoted Him. This was received like a river of inspiration through Margaret's pained, sore, bruised heart, touching every sore point with a gentle finger of silver. It was like a river of inspiration containing silver, gold and other precious metals. God spoke to this prophetess as a Father would speak to his child. Margaret felt extremely close to her heavenly Father.

It was a word of encouragement that would become pillars of steel in a frail frame. This was the ointment that the suffering body, soul and spirit required. Every word fitted neatly into every ache and each void was filled with light coming from each word spoken as a token. This was Margaret's best Friend, and she Margaret must listen as the scholar being taught, and as the drowning man being coaxed out of danger.

'You have clung to the promises of God,' said the Lord, suggesting that as a child will cling to its mother for protection and feeding, there had been this nature of clinging in believing what the Lord had said. 'Like Ivy clings to a wall you have clung to Me.' Ivy always takes hold of every nook and cranny, making each its home.

There seemed to be nothing between Margaret and God as she held on to what God had said and what He would say. To this struggling saint these words were as milk and honey from the Promised Land. Here was the Lord drawing pictures of grace in majesty and colouring them with grace and the green from the grass of Psalm 23.

The Lord spoke on . . . 'You have clung to the Rock, through hardships that have devastated your soul.' Even though it was a smooth surfaced rock, she had managed to find fissures that she could be planted in and grow on into the glory of God. Here was the God of all nature who understood the nature of one. The greatness of God is not seen in trees, sun, moon and flowers, but in knowing the individual as if they were the only one who existed in this world. That explosion of greatness was seen in a soul, a saint holding on to what the Lord had declared. The truth is it held on to her! God was speaking to His favourite thing — a human soul in need of help. He had come on a mission of deliverance to this poor woman who had cried unto the Lord, and that same Lord was delivering her out of all distress, and placing her into rest.

The Lord continued, 'You have clung on to Me even though your suffering has brought you to Jordan's River.' Suffering will always make you feel that you are going to flow away and lose everything, when the truth is that at the other side of the Jordan is the Promised Land. The promise was that Margaret would not sink beneath the waters without trace! Do not look for Moses to take you in! He never went into the Promised Land. He must leave you on the banks of the river. Thank God when He brings us there; we do not have to swim across or row our boat without an anchor. God causes the Jordan to part, and we walk on in that made dry by the word of His mouth. 'Even through the darkest night you have eventually looked up and seen the Morning Star.' Thank God for the stars in a dark night which bring us hope of a better future in a fairer land. When that comes from above it is to make us look up. In the darkness, naturally you would see darkness, but in God the heavens open and we see by faith beyond the dark into the realm of the stars that declare the handiwork of the Creator. It must not be the darkness that enters our soul it must be the glitter and glory of the stars belonging to a heavenly body.

'I saw your knuckles whiten as you clung on to the promises of God,' knuckles that seemed to be wasted in whiteness. The knuckles were white because an enemy was trying to wrest those promises from her heart as all strength and capability was put into resisting. Fingers were being used in emergency. As we reach out, God will come the larger part of the way and cover the gap between Him and you. Nothing keeps a promise like the human heart wrapped around it. All Margaret's efforts had gone into keeping hold of what the Lord had given to her. 'You believed in your heart that you would see the goodness of the Lord in the land of the living.' This had nothing to do with dying; only living and seeing many days.

'You have thought within yourself many times that you were finished.' The end can be mistaken for the beginning; the stop can mean a fresh start. The workings of God are never finished, they are constantly being written into every life. When He pauses it is to introduce another realm, a higher realm. The setting sun can suggest the rising moon. We need wise discernment to hear and understand what the Lord is saying. 'There are still goals for you to go through at each corner of the field.'

The field Margaret saw was marked out like a football field, suggesting that as the line-marker marks out the football field, so the Lord maps out our life before we kick our first ball, or breathe our first intake of breath. You cannot play football without wind being in the ball, and you cannot serve the Lord without a fresh breath of the Spirit, Acts 2:2. The field was marked out by God, and the lines were drawn around its playing area. The Lord decides 'where' and 'what', 'when' and 'why'. The measure of each life is in the hands of the Lord. If the lines require shortening or lengthening He is well able to do either, both or neither. The goals are placed in every life by the Master, and He grants us the ability to score those goals in our achievements. God knows when to blow the whistle for the commencement and the conclusion. You will never leave the field until He decides it is time. In God there are no limits, only open goals through which you can score again and again. There was not one goal but four, one in each corner of the field. You can be a success in a small corner if you have a large heart. 'There will be enough and to spare to such a degree that the fountains of the deep within your own heart will burst open, because of His goodness and providence.'

There is always more within when the Lord pours into our soul. That soul is expanded into another realm, and from that realm we can commence again in God. 'You will prostrate yourself at the feet of your Saviour and Lord.' Every experience no matter how holy, true or rich should leave you prostrate at the feet of Jesus. 'He that is down need fear no fall,' and from that position of being at the Master's feet, there is only one way to go and that is up as He grants the shine of His countenance upon you in grace and peace. At His feet you are made to look up, and as you look up, there is that beautiful Face (the kindest face in the human race) to be gazed upon as a rare glimpse of glory. Being at the feet in full surrender does not mean His feet will walk all over you. It means that there you can discern which way the feet are going and you can follow. Footprints clearly seen lead to destination, declaration and dedication. If those feet should tread on you, it is only that you may receive His imprints into your soul. The Lord continued speaking . . . 'When you arise you will carry an abundance of His glory and again be fruitful.' There comes a moment to fall at His feet but there is also the hour when you must get up and let the Lord of love and glory work out His plan of action in your life. When that happens, the fruit that you bear will be sweet, very sweet to His taste.

The outcome of the consolations of God poured into the soul is that you might understand that it is one thing for you to have God, but it is an entirely different thing for God to have you, body, soul and spirit. It includes all thought, desires, decisions and missions. So much of you needs to surrender as a flag to the wind — so much of you surrendered that there is nothing left for temptation to squeeze, hurt and bend to breaking point.

After these words, Margaret felt nerved to face anything in the coming days, months and years. There is something so strengthening when the Lord speaks into our own situation, and we feel, having been sicker than the proverbial parrot, despite dreadful sickness, we can step out of that sickness and into the health of the Lord.

19

THE ROARING
LION OF JUDAH

Margaret saw in the Spirit the church of Jesus
Christ weak, barely resembling what the Lord had
meant it to be. What should have been strong and
brave, as mighty as any army with banners, was
viewed as that which had been attacked, defeated
and had surrendered to the power of the enemy.

When you look into the church you sometimes
see that wasted as the apostle Paul wasted it as a
wild boar wasting the undergrowth, Acts 8:3. It is
depicted as a vineyard, but it seems, through sense
and time, as if the vines have been wasted, as if a
garden of roses has been turned into a wilderness.
What God has said of His church, describing it
as a bride, is sometimes seen as a divorced bride,
weeping and deserted by her lover.

The army has become a group of renegade
deserters, a rabble thrown together to get their

own way. Even in the metaphor of the sheep in the fold, it can seem to the human spirit as if the ninety and nine are on the hillside lost, while the one is within the fold, Matthew 18:12, 13. If the Church is a building as seen in Ephesians 2:20, 21, that building is in a bad state of repair, it's walls thrown down, as in the Book of Nehemiah and Ezra rather than in the New Testament, where Jesus said, 'I will build my church,' Matthew 16:18. The walls have been broken down as the walls of Jerusalem were. The gates are wide open and the enemy comes and goes as he pleases. The church is a body but that body is sick with sores all over it, like the sickness of Job, and it is in need of the Great Physician to do His healing work.

The cry of Margaret's heart when she saw these things was 'Who will come to the aid of the church?' The answer was not in personalities, preachers or programmes, there are so many of these yet the church still has a great need. The answer wasn't in having more musicians and better programmes. Maybe if the church was re-organised it would then become strong? Margaret realised that it was not organisation that the church required, not even original principles interpreted in a modern society would fully meet the need. God would have to rend the heavens and come down, Isaiah 64:1. If you need carpenters you go to the carpenter. If you require that which is electrical mending you call the electrician. If your sink is overflowing with water and you have an abundance of fountains because of holes in the pipe you call for the plumber. If the church has a great need then it needs to call upon the Lord. He will become the 'Healer' and 'Fixer' of all things spiritual and natural.

Was the answer for God to raise up another world-wide evangelist? Or a sweeping revival? Would the answer be found in better preaching or greater worship? All these thoughts passed through Margaret's mind as a train going through a dark tunnel, but the darkness prevailed and the light at the end of the tunnel was never reached. There was no final destination, only station after station of questions and doubts about the future of the church of Jesus Christ.

It was the month of May 2003, and the whole day was opening up as rose petals under the coaxing of nature. The place where Margaret was praying was so quiet it could be described as the resting place of dew. The quietness seemed to calm everything in the prayer room; even the ticking of the clock seemed quieter.

The church of Jesus Christ was weighing on her mind. What could a woman do to help in this dire situation? Maybe she should pray and in doing so ask the Lord to intervene. The words had no sooner entered her head when suddenly there was a loud roar of a lion as if it had been disturbed whilst eating its prey. It was not the size or shape of the lion with its golden mane that seemed to stand out, but its blood curdling voice. This surpassed the blowing of the wind, sound of rain, creaking of the tree branch or thunderous roll of the storm.

It took Margaret completely by surprise. It wasn't the roar of a lion seeking prey or attacking the prey for it would not make such a noise. This lion was out for the kill, but not in human understanding or definition. It was the multiplied shout that grabbed her attention like nothing else had ever done. The voice filled every corner of the room, leaving no space for any other sound. Margaret's ear drums were 'drummed' by the roar of the lion.

This was the voice supreme that quietened other voices. What the sergeant major on parade will do with his voice so the lion was doing as it roared, as if roaring everything else into submission. It was the roar of command. It was not a call for help, but a signal that something was on the attack, and would not cease until satisfied. The challenge was in the roar of the lion daring anything else to dare!

This was the noise of the Lion of the Tribe of Judah who meant business. Instead of blowing a trumpet in Zion, God was sending the roar of the lion as a challenge for others to keep off His sacred territory the church. It was the roar of the king of the jungle advising and commanding all to take their hands off what belonged to the Lion. In that loud roar, He was making His claim to be the Lord of the Church. It was such a roar sounding like thunder and then a cataract of water as it streams over a sheer drop. Thunder can force fruit to fall from trees and make cows give birth because of the great noise, Psalm 29:9. All heard this voice. It was shrill and yet it was full. It was loud but as distinctive as any trumpet call or 'big bang theory'!

Margaret had never heard a sound like this before. The voice was more radiant than a fireworks display. It was so loud, bold and fierce she thought the timbers of the house could and should have been ripped apart by the roar. It was the sort of roar that could have rolled away the stone at the resurrection of Jesus Christ. Anything within the sound of that roar knew that the Lion meant business. They would remain where they were at their own peril. This roar was His calling card! Margaret did not run in her spirit but decided to wait on the Lord of the loud.

Jesus Christ had come to claim what was His own. There were evil forces and that had taken the church to leave it in the lurch, to destroy and kill it, and this roar was a declaration of war. What had been held captive was taken into captivity. Within this new captivity would be freedom, not the freedom of dying and escaping but the freedom of entering into a new kingdom and experiencing a new rule on earth, with the freedom to go where the voice had gone before. It would be like the voice of John the Baptist who cried before the Lord, Matthew 3:3, filling every valley and smoothing out the rough and tough places, as grace was poured out and poured in.

Margaret could see the Lord coming out of His place. He was on the move, and when He moves all before Him must move, run for shelter or turn for help in their dilemma. God was on a rescue mission not for the blind, the halt or the deaf but for those held captive within His church. He would come as a mighty Lion of valour to rescue the perishing and care for the dying. He would do what lions do not normally do — rescue, not destroy. Lions do not normally roar into a situation to rescue that which is within their allotted territory.

Here was a Lion that was going to rescue lambs! Here was a small part of the millennium reign where the lion and the lamb will lie down together, Isaiah 11:6.

The enemy had been into the church and had sown seeds of doubt, despair and sickness. It was like the parable of the enemy who had sown tares instead of wheat whilst it was dark, Matthew 13:25 – 27. It was this enemy that was about to be dealt with. Hypocrisy would be the first thing to be dealt with by the roaring, roaming, rushing lion.

That which was troubling the church at this

time would be brought to its knees even as it had sought to bring the people of God to their knees. He thought to do it with sickness, disease, terror and torment, but the saints had been forced to their knees to pray. From the sickness suffered healing would spring up as an antidote to their malady. The lion would come to them with claws filled with healing ointment, and great strength, the strength of the roaring Lion of Judah would enter into them. His flowing mane would be long and strong, and they would take hold of it to be carried through and out. There was a place in that mane for every believer to hide. There would be a personal resurrection for each. All the people had to do was to follow the sound of the voice to its source.

The rage of the Lion would be directed against Satan and all his hordes, even as multitudes of blessings would come to the people of God. It sounded as if the Lion was in a fury, yet it was part of a devised plan, for there is no place where He fears to rush in. We are not dealing with an angel but the God of the angel armies, 'The Lord of Hosts'.

This Lion of the Tribe of Judah had no need to call others to be His assistant. This Lion of the Tribe of Judah was a lone walker, worker and stalker as it came against the enemy of the believer. That voice and lion shape was enough to crush, bend and break, destroy and kill other influences. This was more than the scattering of a few leaves in the wind or the multiplying of dust thrown into the air. There was strength and strategy in that roar. It was not roaring for effect, but roaring as one shouts before entering the final battle. No preacher or personality would rout the enemy. The enemy would be usurped by the Lion.

Jesus, in the shape of a Lion and with the voice of command as found in 1 Thessalonians 4:17, 18, had come Himself to rout the enemy and fight for His bride. The challenge was great, the prize was noble and above many rubies.

Surrounding the church was a hedge that had thick brambles leading into and from it. No one could enter it or leave the centre without being severely punished by those out reaching branches. They were so large that they appeared as antlers. They were there to safeguard what the enemy had taken into captivity. There was no way out and no way in. How would the Lion get within these rearing antlers? Would it be by taking the thorns upon His head in the shape of a crown? Would the roaring lion descend from the sky and land in the middle of them to claim what was His?

A key was needed that could unlock torment and despair. That key was not metal or wooden but was in the roar, the majestic roar of the Lion. As the Lord came forth as a roaring lion, the roar caused the earth to quiver, and large fissures opened up as it began to quake at the sound of His voice. The earth began to rock to and fro like a drunken man on a windy day, swaying and unsteady, thinking that the world around him was moving, whilst he was standing still.

As the earth began to break open, leaving gaping holes as large as hell itself without the fire, attended by particles of flying dust, the antler sized brambles were uprooted unceremoniously and tossed into the air, as if a cat was playing with a mouse. The thick hedge was in full view as Margaret waited with bated breath to see what the Lion would do next. The thick hedge surrounding the church was turned upside down the roots in the air, and brambles flying along in the wind. It was better than a farmer with a plough going through the field. What seemed like chaos was organised by the roar of this Lion. Every bramble branch uprooted was marked by the roar of the Lion. This magnificent beast was marking its territory with a roar.

The moment the hedge was uprooted, the church that had been so maligned began to prosper. Room had been made for growth and expression. Where evil had multiplied, grace began to abound. Those held in bondage had been set free to express themselves in their calling. The restricted had become unrestricted; the dead made alive, the sorry prisoners were being turned into saints.

Margaret could see the church worldwide, and

when the brambles were uprooted the churches began to flourish. Small churches that had been insignificant began to increase in number, until they became a numberless company with numberless blessings. The prodigal sons began returning to these churches, they began to express themselves as those who had been set free to be free.

Mother churches began to stir, dissatisfied with what had happened in the past. They felt they must mother babies that would be born by the move of the Spirit of the Lord. They began to go over the wall, and reach out for the lost with aching hearts. They had full breasts that needed to be emptied as babies began to be born. The converts not only reached out, they brought in.

These churches were so successful that they had to hire mega buildings to house the converts. The mentality of the small sheep pen had gone forever. The 'little flock' had become a mighty force. They eventually had to hire stadia to house those who wanted to join with them in glorifying the Lord. This was revival on a glorious scale, brought about in the heat of the Lion's call and command.

The terraces in the stadium were filled with people. The same crowds that had gone to the football match had now come to Jesus Christ. A spirit of rejoicing had entered into God's people, they were not singing they were worshipping-you could not stop them; they required no human leader. What was in the church had been taken onto the streets, into the thoroughfare and into the shopping malls. They began to sing the songs of the Spirit. As the gates opened to admit the crowds, so they began to sing song after song, not from a song sheet but that given there and then by the Spirit of God. Each person was becoming an orchestra, playing a symphony of praise unto God.

The Spirit of God moved over the people wave after wave as they worshipped. As one song faded, another began as an offering of incense to the Lord on the throne. These people were the creators of their own songs. One would commence singing and then the whole crowd would sing the same song. The singing began in one place, and then went to another, as if the waves of the Spirit were washing over the saints of God. They were in perfect harmony. Here was a College of Music with the Holy Spirit as Tutor in truth to bring into tune! It was so powerful.

Those Mother churches that did not increase in number became a hive of activity with worship that can only be described as heavenly; they sang a new song unto the Lion. The churches that did not establish pioneer churches began to send out people far and wide that took the heart of the Mother church with them into the far flung corners of the earth. They sent forth those locally, nationally and internationally to spread the word. This was a glorious display of resurrection power brought about by the roar of the Lion of the Tribe of Judah.

I could hear rumblings on earth and in heaven as if the Lion of the Tribe of Judah had been to earth and was ascending back into heaven until all churches become one Church under His power, and all enemies would bow at His feet. The Lord had triumphed in the cause of the church of Jesus Christ.

20

CONSECRATION
AS CEREMONY

Margaret felt she had to seek the Lord on behalf of a local church in the Manchester area of England. The history and spirituality of this group of people was well known to her. They were highly organised, so organised that if you let a sweet paper fall before it reached the ground someone had been trained to catch it. Whatever need arose someone was given the task of stepping in and meeting that need. This church lived, moved and had its being in organisation, and it was a successful church. If you think that organisation does not pay you should visit the church the Lord was speaking to Margaret about.

In her spirit all the facts were laid out for her to see and act upon so that she might pray for them. Here in her mind, as revealed by the Lord, was all that was mechanical yet it lacked the oil. This church was like Noah's ark, every plank of wood in place, the animals of God's choice within the building, but the ark did not sail, it stayed where it was. It was like an orchestra playing instruments yet no music sounded. The instruments were highly polished but that did nothing for the music.

Margaret began to pray, and the Spirit of the Lord took her back into the past history of the steam train. As a girl she had lived near the railway station in Wakefield, West Yorkshire, England. As children they had played the fanciful game that if you were the first to see a green train or a green engine then that brought good luck. As a child she had gone onto the local station to admire the latest steam machines that travelled the length and breadth of the country. Often the thought had been wrestled with: what kept the train on the lines? Why did the engine driver sound the whistle? On a cold morning why did the wheels seem to slip and race forwards and then backwards, the wheels moving so quickly the engine did not follow. Then in her childish mind she wondered where all the steam went that came out of the engine, and why it disappeared immediately it appeared. Although the engines were so big, powerful and speedy, why did they sometimes appear to be late and never run to time? To a young child these were profound thoughts.

There was the realisation in the prophecy that the Lord communicated into her spirit that in God nothing is lost. He will take childhood memories and teenage concerns, what we learn when we are young and pretty or old and grey, and use these experiences as a paintbrush to paint pictures of spirituality and declension you can understand, and that those listening can also understand. If the weather is fair or foul, those things that happen around the oak tree become part of the tree, and nothing is wasted, all works together for the good of nature and human beings, and in particular those who love the Lord. Poets have suggested that sounds coming from a burning log are like the sweet conversations between lovers who have sat on the log in the past.

Margaret felt as if she had just passed through a history lesson, what was conveyed to her by the Spirit of the Lord was going to be used. What seemed a mystery would be revealed. What seemed like a jaunt down memory lane would become quite clear in the next hour.

Suddenly Margaret could see one of the steam engines she had seen and admired as a child. The natural thing was to wonder what relevance that had to do with the church she was praying about. Now was not the time for taking a train and going on a holiday.

Most trains run on oil or electricity today, steam engines are a thing of the past. This was a magnificent, highly polished engine that she could see in the Spirit. The engine driver polished it with loving strokes as if he never wanted it to perish. It looked as if it had been polished in oil, the paintwork was pristine, the metal work sublime. The spirit of the child visiting the British Rail museum in York, England, entered into her spirit. This was an exciting thing to behold, she felt like a school child on a day trip viewing the engine they had come to see. They had come to view the one that was the fastest steam train, like the 'Flying Scotsman' or the 'Mallard'. This certainly was not a replica of Stephenson's 'Rocket'! When Stephenson built it, being the first train they said that it would never start, and if it did start it would never stop! The creator was wasting his time and heading for disaster.

The train was beautiful to look at. Beauty was in the eye of the beholder. The whistle sounding, the engine began to spit water onto the track, the fire was burning, and even the coal that was to be fed to the fire was shining as if painted with glory. Only the best oil, paint, steel and carvings had been used in the creation of this engine. The wheels of the engine were moving backwards and forwards, but the train itself did not move. Margaret began to wonder why. With that power and a head of steam, with the latest machinery and the best engine driver in the cab, it was going nowhere. It was as wasted as a snowflake in a hot fire. This was proving to be a mystery. So much power and so little movement. The power of the fire and water turned to steam was not being engaged to the carriages that the train was wanting to pull along the track and out of the station.

The thought crossed Margaret's mind as a swallow might skim the surface of the water, 'Did this train with all its potential and beauty think it had been created to be an exhibition? Was it the first train, created never to leave the station?' The public had purchased their tickets, and demanded that the train should travel over the hill and far away into the rest of God's creation. Margaret began to understand what the word 'stationary' meant as seen in this beautiful creation, this masterpiece that was in danger of becoming a fossil!

The Lord pointed to the railway lines made out of the best steel, laid to gauge and leading out of the station. The sun caught hold of them, and a silver light reflected from them as the sun shone. Margaret didn't want to be dazzled by the railway lines or the highly polished engine, so she put her hand to her eyes to act as a shield from the brightness of beauty that was not to be. As the Lord pointed to the tracks, He began to speak to His handmaiden. It is when we let the Lord do the talking that the greatest revelations come. The Lord spoke and Margaret listened.

'These tracks you are looking at seem to be ordinary tracks built of steel and held together with sleepers and large metal pieces, but they are more than that. These tracks represent the dedication of former generations who have brought the church to what should be its finest hour only to find that it has been turned into a faltering moment. These tracks have been laid in blood, sweat and tears at great cost, including the cost of a Life that was laid down so these people might get out of the church, get out of the station, that the church might go somewhere and do something.' The pioneer spirit of this church was missing. It only existed for itself. These tracks had been measured by God, and laid as godly principles to get a church on the move. 'These tracks are the 'way' that I have laid down, so that anyone wanting to leave the station might move from station to their destination.' There is a right way and there is a wrong way. Travel the wrong way and you will be shunted onto another line that comes to a dead end. Go the way the Lord has laid before you, and you will travel an endless track that leads to glory. As a train moves out of the station it touches county after county in England, and then it moves from country to country. Wherever it goes and however fast it travels, the track dictates where it should go.

The church that will move out of the station and reach out into other areas will never lack the track. They will never lack the leading of the Lord who wants us to realise and release our full potential. The engine was built to move swiftly and go from area to area. Without tracks, without what God has said, the train will not move. Had this church forgotten the great commission, Mark 16:15? It required the spirit of the pioneers to stock up the fire to produce the steam, and then to glide out of the station.

At that moment the voice of God went silent, and Margaret wondered why. The vision was cut off when it began to get interesting. There are times when the Lord only gave Margaret part of the story, and then later, sometimes even years later, complete story. Margaret felt sad when the picture disappeared and the voice ceased, as if the book had been closed by an unseen hand, and the seals could not be opened. She did not want the train to be left in the station with so much ability going into steam waste.

The months went by as Margaret pondered all of these things in her heart and wondered what they all meant. She had received a revelation that would sustain her as winter days dragged on, merging dawn into darkness with nothing between, only what the Lord had revealed. In the waiting time all that had been witnessed was heightened until a sense of the expectancy of a coming answer entered into her spirit. Some things are better when left to mature into fullness. Cheese or wine is left to mature so that they can come together to bless the palate. If you are satisfied with part, then you will only have a part, but if you wait God's time you will receive God's reasoned explanation.

Margaret felt that the Lord must be consulted by asking Him what this meant. He was the Giver and He must be the Interpreter.

As prayer was made, the picture of the steam engine re-emerged into the room until the picture filled it to capacity, Then as this servant of the Almighty turned to closer inspect, finding out the finer details and to know the difference between cloth, garment, needle work, steam and steel, Margaret saw three men standing on the platform. These men were attired in British Rail standard uniform although one had more oil on his clothes than the other two. They were people with a task to perform and a mission to enter.

The Spirit of God began to whisper into Margaret's heart: 'One is the driver, one is the stoker, the other the engineer.' It is their combined effort that will get the glossy train from the station and take it from the north to the south, and east to west of England.

The message was for the leadership of this church. It was a message to the driver, stoker and engineer. If they would listen things would happen. The polished engine would no longer be a show-piece it would be turned into a masterpiece. This 'iron horse' would move at such speed it would be difficult to trace its sleek movements. Such a heavy thing made out of metal but moving swiftly and forward into its destination, carrying others with it.

These three men, led by the Spirit of God, and having more anointing upon them than on their oily rag, could get the church to move along the right lines. When those in charge of the church welcome Father, Son and Holy Spirit, there would be such a surge of power, a steam engine with a 'head of steam'. They then would be going somewhere and taking others with them. This train would carry people from near and far to their desired destiny. In the Trinity was the power of the engine. In the Godhead was the power to move the church. All the power at their disposal would be harnessed for accomplishment.

Margaret began to rub her eyes and touch her ears because what she was seeing and hearing rocked her emotions, ears and eyes. As a child she rubbed her eyes when she couldn't believe what she was seeing. Was she hearing things too wonderful for men to hear? Margaret began to ask the Lord, 'What will be the signs of their surrender? How shall I know they have submitted themselves unto Your authority?

The forthcoming revival would happen according to the will and wishes of God and not men. Margaret knew God had a timetable, even as British Rail had theirs.

The leaders of the church were very good at organising metal into a steam engine form, but when they had done everything for lasting growth and achievement they required something more.

Engines need to be engines, and exhibit what they were manufactured for! A train must triumph as a train, because as it had been it was no better than a wheelbarrow!

God began to hand to Margaret the blueprint that could be recognised so that she would know when the church was moving in the right direction, and when it would cease from becoming a mere showpiece.

'These signs shall follow them that surrender', so said God. The elderly who had felt 'put down' and rejected would be used by the Lord. These older folk would become seed corn. They would begin to bear fruit more than they had ever done in previous years, fulfilling the promise of God. 'They shall bear fruit in old age.' Their bones, tibia, fibula, ankles and knees, would be strengthened as they were lengthened to fulfil the vision. Old age would not become a by word for 'uselessness'. These would not be old bones buried in the ground by a stray dog. Their days would be more than their strength. Back bones would be strengthened to enable them to be capable for the task that the Lord would call them into. The weak would say they were strong because they were strong.

Each part of the fulfilment of what the Almighty was saying would be dependent on the word given and received being allowed to operate into its fullness of dispensation. Young people would be baptised in the Holy Spirit. Those as young as eight would prophesy in the church, and what they prophesied would be acceptable. This would be the 'acceptable year of the Lord'.

God would not leave any age out of His fatherhood. The Ancient of Days would cater for all ages at all stages. The middle aged people who had lifted a flag to encourage others to go on, and had supported the church financially to preach the gospel, would rise up as prodigals returning from a far country. They would be as those who awake first thing in the morning rubbing their eyes because of the things they would see, because they couldn't believe what they were witnessing. They would be refreshed as grass in the morning, having grown in the night, refreshed by the morning dew. They would rise up in indignation because of the state of the world, doing exploits in the name of the Lord.

As the leaders obeyed Father, Son and Holy Spirit, that train would leave the station less polished but with more grip on the tracks. It would speed along, and many who had never thought of the church before would want to ride on this train. They would not simply be there for the ride but the for the many miles it would travel influencing others. It would become a copy for other evangelical churches. The church would be on the move, powerful, forward looking, because it had not lost its interest in people. The blessing received would not be turned inwards. All the signals would be on 'go'; there would be no red lights, no end of track experience, no shunting from one track to another. It would stop to welcome new converts, or to allow missionaries get to off the train at stations appointed by the Lord.

21

EXPECTING THE UNEXPECTED

Margaret often travelled to Canada with Terry, and no matter which country in the world they were in Margaret found that God is the same. The clouds, sky, sun moon and stars of any nation are part of the creative and productive power of God, Romans 1:20. The power that is witnessed in creation needs to come via the Holy Spirit to save, set free, satisfy and heal. There is no place we can go where God is not. The power of God has been witnessed in every nation; there are no barriers or borders to His ability to heal the sick, open the eyes of the blind and cast out demons. The promise to Abraham was that his seed would be as the sand on the seashore and as the stars in the sky, making every nation part of the working power of God, Genesis 22:17; 26:4; 32:12.

Margaret was as much a servant of the Lord in her own country as she was in any country. It may seem more difficult to believe on home soil, because we begin to trust those things that we can see, and the familiar things of life can displace faith. It is easier to believe when we have nothing else to trust in. When the tree has only one branch the bird does not have a great choice of where to rest. Wherever there was a need in others, there was a need in Margaret Atkinson to seek God, to pray and ask the Lord to step in and help. When God steps in, it is but a small step that He takes yet it is a huge leap, a giant step for mankind, in our faith.

Whenever we pray for the sick we are taking creation back to the Creator with more confidence than you would take a broken watch to a watch-maker. One involves the mechanical while praying for the sick involves the Creator of all things, part of the 'all things bright and beautiful' that the Lord created.

A black lady stood at the front of the meeting, she was about twenty eight years of age. There was no indication of what she was suffering or what the Almighty was going to do. Jehovah rarely sends a herald to tell what is going to happen. It is enough that Scripture says so, and it is so. Such is the nature of the Lord that He just says and it is so, He commands and it stands faster than that described as granite, Psalm 33:9. That is why in the New Testament so often the word 'suddenly' is used, Mark 9:8. Luke 2:13.Acts 2:2; 9:3; 16:26.

As her eyes met Margaret's there was a look of

pain in those eyes, shadows had formed across her cheek bones to reveal a suffering face. Suffering had used this face as a canvas. Ruth was like an animal trapped in a snare unable to extricate itself, suffering while in the snare causing deep wounds that were now festering.

Ruth had joined the row of wounded soldiers at the cross as she came forward for prayer. As she gazed at Margaret praying for others, there was the look of hope in her eyes. Although she had suffered, that suffering had not reduced her pain or the trust that she had in the living, healing God. Ruth had been like someone who had fallen into a river, the waters swirling around her, and about to sink, but the hope that someone would throw her a lifeline had never diminished. This could be the moment when she would be rescued to run the race of life. Catastrophe and calamity could be turned into consolation.

Faith was larger than the need in her body, soul or spirit. There was that in the centre of the pain calling, begging, pleading with the Lord to do something for her. If tears could be measured and weighed then these tears would weigh much. Here was the liquid of the soul poured through eyes. If only the pain and the longing could be measured!

Ruth stood before Margaret with a heart that was reaching out for a miracle. The longing could never be satisfied with anything else, even prayer or promise, but had to be met by the living, healing, helping God. One sweep of His Hand and all would be helped, all would be healed.

This was not the time for a mirage or 'mumbo-jumbo' — what was required must be as real as the ground this seeker stood on. Here was a miracle seeker coming to the God who is a Miracle Worker. Was she the last one in the queue? As she arrived would the shutter come down, and a notice be posted 'business closed'? Would God run out of the things that He creates miracles from? These along with other doubtful, dismal thoughts were on the tip of Ruth's tongue.

She required one of the 'signs' and 'wonders' that had been promised in Mark 16:17. The preacher had said that the Lord could do anything, and part of that 'anything' was the centre of the pain of her plight. Ruth was like somebody trying to reach the top of a very high wall without a ladder to assist.

That word promised throughout all ages needed to be 'confirmed' by the power of God. Margaret knew, through her theological training, that the word 'confirm' in 1 Kings 1:14 means 'to fill up or out'. In the New Testament in Mark 16:20 it suggests 'to make firm, strong or sure'. Ruth required that which would give her the 'power' to be healed. It is always good to get something 'new' from the New Testament such as 'new' wine, 'new' tongues and a 'new' body part.

Ruth had an aching pain in her back, which must be released. Although she had been prayed for before, nothing had happened. Maybe it was because 'ordinary' prayers had been offered. A word had been spoken over her that was not mixed with faith? The prayers offered had not bettered her, but rather had left her with remorse and doubt feeding on her misgivings, Mark 5:26. There was no extraordinary 'sign' that had entered Ruth's body as a 'sign' of healing. Sigh and sight still replaced 'sign'. Every day remained every day, but now she wanted the pattern of things to be broken. The end of the pattern of things as they were must be given to the Almighty. Commencing from that given, He would create a new pattern according to His power. Ruth was always left saying 'Where is the Lord God of Elijah'. 'If the Lord be God then why have all these things befallen us?'

Suddenly hope took hold of desperation, and in the face of this child of God was the plea of a child asking a parent for food because that child was in danger of starving to death! What had suggested defeat was suddenly turned into joy and release. Margaret was here to pray for the sick, that they might be released to be what they had been created for. The old pattern of pain must be broken into many pieces, and scattered into the blowing wind.

As Margaret laid hands on Ruth, the story was told of how this condition had entered into her life. What had been bright and young, vivacious and desirable had been attacked by an enemy. This woman was like a doctor's notebook and required a prescription for healing that would never be written by a doctor's computer. The doctor's notebook had stayed open at one page, and the symptoms would be repeated again and again. Here was a casebook without a prescription that would not produce lasting healing and health.

Margaret gently took her on one side and asked Ruth to tell her about her need. It was a story mingled with pain and signed with suffering. 'I was playing on a rubbish dump as a child', so Ruth began her story. Margaret was thinking 'What a place to start a life, on a rubbish dump!' Fragrant roses grow on rubbish dumps! Then Margaret realised that God takes the beggar from the dunghill and seats him among princes, 1 Samuel 2:8 (quoted by another woman of God's kind dealings) referring to the eastern beggar sitting on a heap of dung, begging from a prince, who doesn't just give a gift, but takes him into the palace. That piece of camel dung brings him to the same height as the prince riding a horse or a camel, and they are then able to communicate as equals. The greater the dirt the more the beggar comes into contact with the prince. What could be greater than being brought into the presence of the Prince of Peace?

Ruth continued 'I found a large refrigerator

door lying on the ground, and I thought it would be a good thing to play with. It was not attached to the main cabinet, so I thought it would make a nice shelter or maybe it could be turned into a den? Then I tried to lift the door from where it was. It was heavier and larger than I thought. As I lifted it, the large metal object fell on me, and as it fell my back was wrenched, and a searing pain went down my back, and left me stuttering and shuddering. The pain was like a roaring fire. The steel door knocked me to the ground where I was left encased in pain.'

The fridge door had knocked the health out of this body and replaced it with pain and despair. It had done its worst and now God would do His best. This was a case for the Great Physician. When the Lord heals, it can be as if it never happened, wiped off the page of life. Jesus as a carpenter had taken broken bits of wood and made something from them, and He would now work a miracle through this flesh by the power of the Lord. Here the throne of God would be established where pain had ruled supreme. This church would become the Carpenter's bench.

'After the fridge door had fallen on me I was in constant pain, and had to take pain killers on a daily basis. I experienced 'trial by tablet'! These pain killers never removed the pain, they simply made it more bearable. I have been in pain morning, noon and night. There has been this steel lump of pain that I have been walking in. I want you, Margaret to pray for me, and ask God to remove the pain, and heal my body, so that I can move freely. The pain has made the hours, days, weeks, months and years seem longer.'

Margaret laid hands on her, believing that 'they shall lay hands on the sick and they shall recover,' Mark 16:18. It was a simple but sure prayer. There are some pains that only prayer can remove. There was the conviction that the tormenting pain would fall from Ruth's back, and return to the Fall brought about by Adam when he sinned in the Garden of Eden. How can pain be described? It is a torment, a feeling, a frustration, an instrument of war sticking into your flesh. It is a real thorn in the flesh as a wooden stake driven into your heart. It is a sense of not being able to move without this enemy tormenting you with hot irons. It is not the pain of loss or grief only in that it is a feeling of something missing, something in your body that cannot be removed. It can be like the Roman torture of tying a dead corpse to a living man, and leaving the dead corpse to eat into the flesh of the living. Who would deliver her from this body of death? Romans 7:24. Here another king had established his kingdom of pain, pain and more pain. There was always more where that came from!

Ruth wanted to demonstrate what God had done in her, and without any suggestion from Margaret she began to demonstrate that she had been healed. It was as dynamic as it was delightful because it was in a way that was not expected. It was one of those rare sights that could be placed in the annals of 'unusual happenings' to Christians. Margaret was expecting Ruth to bend forward to see if the pain was still in her lower back, but to Margaret's astonishment Ruth immediately bent over backwards, as if she was a rainbow after a storm or a bridge over a River of Sighs.

This was no shrug of the shoulders; it was not just a slight bend to see if it was alright to twist. It was the full application of faith. Ruth reached back and touched the floor with her hands while her feet remained anchored! If there was any pain, what Ruth was doing would increase that pain, and do further damage to her back. It was as if her body, in an act of worship, was bending backwards to go into the days when Ruth had been happy and well. After all, people do not bend over backwards as a testimony to healing; they usually bend forward as if worshipping the God who heals, yielding to Him in an act of worship and dedication. Ruth was 'bending backwards' to help the Almighty who had helped her. While people are bent forwards or backwards there is always the prayer that they might scoop up some of the love of God from that position.

Ruth was reaching backwards as if wanting to leave the past in the past, telling the pain that had tormented her with a relish that its kingdom was now broken. As she bent backwards she was letting the pain go back to where it belonged. As she stood upright with a sunny smile, pain was left where it belonged, on the floor to be buried forever. Ruth would join the list of those who have been healed, and have gone on to do exploits like those who know their God, Daniel 11:32.

Ruth did not just bend over backwards once or twice, but so many times that it was impossible to count in thankfulness for what the Lord had done. These emotions were the initial evidence of healing. Not only the back had been set free, but also the spirit of the woman to worship God and fall in love with Him and His ways afresh. Ruth felt that as she went back, there she met with Christ who was standing in her shadow, waiting and wanting to heal her. The freedom in this one's life was not in going forward but in going backwards, then the forward march could begin. The miracle began with impossibility and concluded with impossibility, because she had gone backwards and downwards, not forwards and downwards.

Although Ruth went backwards she never fell down, never lost her balance. It seemed as if a firmer Hand was holding her. Margaret had seen gymnasts with trainers standing to the side to make sure they kept their balance, and it was as if this was taking place when Ruth was prayed for.

Ruth shook her shoulders, stood erect, and then began to move around with a look of delight on her face. If she had been given half a kingdom her happiness could not have been greater! She began to exclaim to all the church: 'I am free! The pain has gone! I am healed!' Here was good news that came from the news of the gospel. Here was a herald of freedom from pain received by the power of the Name of Jesus.

God had done His best where an enemy had done the worst to a woman who wanted to serve Him. Pain had been sown in a body like a seed in the soil. God had come to her aid and dealt with the root of her discomfort. Pain could not become part of His plan, that plan did not include pain, worry and stress. This was the dawning of a new day. The lady would be able to do what she had not done for years. The 'works' of the enemy had been destroyed by the grace of God through healing.

22

WHEN DESIRES
ARE SATISFIED

There are certain promises in the Bible that we feel are relate to the spiritual. We think they are divorced from that which is defined as natural and everyday. There is no demarcation of secular and sacred, priest and pew, clergy and laity. Laity must never be devoid of piety, as people should be one in their witness, for all are one in the priesthood of believers. Different gifts operate in different ways, but it is God who gives the gifts, Romans 11:29. There is a misunderstanding of thinking which says there is a difference between priest and person, laity and ministry, and such misunderstanding needs the light of revelation from the Light of the World.

Margaret saw the promises of God as being for the whole of life. Every movement and every moment of each day were part of life in Christ. On the main highway as in the back alley, on a country lane as in a cottage, the promises of God were always promises. They did not change when they found an alteration in circumstances. A cow is a cow whether it is in the field or a milking shed, and should produce milk wherever it is.

What happened to Margaret in any particular day was just a slice of the whole loaf of the daily bread asked for. In the Old King James Version of the Bible, Genesis 47:17, it says that Joseph 'fed them' with bread.' The margin states: 'He 'led' them with bread.' The Bread of Heaven is part of the miraculous nature of God revealed in our lives and seen sometimes as glory. That slice of daily bread can be an answer to prayer; it can be God performing a wonderful miracle, the Lord directing you to the left when you thought it would be better to move to the right.

The gospel, as the God of the gospel, must be at the heart of society. It must be God on the highway and byway, as well as the Lord in the church pew or pulpit, altar or alcove. There must be an ability to recognise the Almighty in the sacred page as well as in prayer or a gift, expected or unexpected.

Nothing happens to the believer by chance, only by the change that the Spirit of God brings into a life. We have desires passed on to us by the Creator, and those things we desire are given to encourage us to seek God for the desire to be met.

The bud must be turned into a rose by a process

of nature, but the Lord works with, above and below nature and natural things. Nature can be taken and converted to being used by the Lord. Whatever happens, the finger and hand of the Lord is at work among His servants. However bad or good, dark or light the circumstances, God can work His will and purpose to bring blessing to those who love Him and would walk in His ways.

There are times when you will feel like Sir Winston Churchill did when the British electorate rejected him and his party after victory over Germany. One American visitor told Churchill that the rejection was 'a blessing in disguise,' to which Churchill replied, 'I must say it is well disguised.'

If you do not remove the shell from the nut then the nut will never be planted. Once it is unwrapped it has potential for growth. There has to be a discovery of what a thing is and what it must be used for, even as your ministry also must be discovered.

Life for Margaret was a constant discovery of the Almighty, and what He had called her to do. She desired to live in the echo of that calling. It may not always be a blast from a trumpet, but nevertheless it must be developed into musical notes, so that anyone hearing the 'sound' from the trumpet would gather themselves together for war. If she had heard the footsteps of the Lord, then she must follow on in the sound of what had been heard, for it could only be the footstep of the Great Shepherd of the sheep leading from the plain to pasture, away from pain into purity.

There were moments in the life of Margaret when normal everyday things entered into her heart as a blessing from the Almighty. Natural happenings might be seen as the product of human thinking, but on reflection these happenings were brought to her by the Spirit of God who knows all, tells all and reveals all. Sometimes what is brought is covered, and only revealed as we begin to act. The word 'manifestation' means 'an uncovering' or an 'unveiling'. All we require is an empty heart ready to be filled. We need to hunger and thirst, for it is the nature of God to fill the hungry with good things and to pour water on him (her) that is thirsty as water on dry ground, Isaiah 44:3.

While walking around a local food store Margaret had a sudden natural desire for a slice of home cooked ham. You might think that all desire for food come from bodily needs, yet here was the Lord planting a desire in order to reveal how He would answer a prayer provoked by desire. He wanted to let the love of God wash over her soul again and again until it became a river of consolation.

Even desiring that which is 'good for food' can come from the Almighty, because through this desire Margaret was taught a spiritual lesson, that the One we serve is with us even when we are shopping. Praying, looking, walking talking — all are part of serving if we have a heart for the Lord. We need to know what is the heart of God for us today. Margaret wanted to walk where He walked, to go where He commanded. If only she could be as a ray of light when God in Genesis had said, 'Let there be light'? That command to follow Him must be followed to the end. Margaret had to decide which part of His heart He wanted to reveal. Wherever and whenever you dip into it, there is a fullness Divine, and some new aspect waiting for you to receive in teaching. There are no shallow parts or shoreline to the love of the Lord. God is not one thing He is many things and all things, as found in Redemption, made to each believer wisdom, righteousness and redemption, 1 Corinthians 1:30.

Margaret's mind was not on spiritual things. I don't think it was on any particular thing as she looked at all the items in the supermarket that she didn't need. Suddenly a great desire filled her heart. It was not to pray, read the Bible or witness, not even to help an aged lady with her basket. It was the desire for a nice thick slice of ham! During her days of pregnancy she had experienced desires for unusual food, such as carrots or cabbage leaves. This time she was not pregnant, only full of the word of God that had been hidden in her heart that Jehovah might not be sinned against. Why was there such a desire for ham in her heart?

She went to the food counter to see if there was any ham on display, for they usually had lovely pieces tempting and reviving fainting hunger. The sight she would see might be enough to fill the longing of the moment. Here was a paradise for hunger as seen in the ham. There were large slices of dead pig in ham form on a shelf, offered for sale. There it was, flat and red, with a price tag sticking out of it like a sail on a ship!

Disappointment written over her face, she turned away because the price was too much. The size of the slices would have choked the pig the ham came from! They were huge slices, and Margaret realised that her digestion system would not cope with a slice that size. In her disappointment she uttered a small prayer where she stood, and it became holy ground. 'Lord provide me with a piece of ham,' she prayed. There and then Margaret sowed a seed of faith, and believed that through her prayer the Lord would give her a nice piece of ham. There must have been some disappointment in her prayer but no delusion, because there was the strong conviction the Almighty was mighty wherever she was, because He was there with her, and that is why as she prayed that prayer, whispering into an ear that always hears, a God that not only understands but interprets every need.

What is a cry or a sob, even a wet tear, is a

trumpet sound to the Lord. The tear becomes a musical note, the voice so eloquent. Turning away from the ham, there was the conviction it had been committed to the Lord, and He would only supply that which was needed. Maybe she didn't need it enough? If only she had a wolf, (a big, good wolf) as in the story of 'The Three Little Pigs' that would huff and puff until the house fell down and then she could have some ham.

Margaret prepared to return home, forgetting about the ham episode. After all, it was only a human desire. Little did she realise that the Lord had not only heard her prayer, and seen the desire but was about to meet the need in greater abundance than anything that could be obtained in a shop.

Those of an atheistic disposition will attempt to translate an answer to prayer into the language of the dumb! These clouds without water try to make God's answer into a 'coincident', then an 'accident', and when this does not satisfy they try to explain it as a 'coincident' — one event happening at the same time as another. They miss the nature and teaching of the Lord has done, and doing by three miles. The sense of encouragement and expectation is missing from their way of thinking.

The Scripture teaches that God raised up Pharaoh for this purpose, Exodus 9:16. If God can reveal His power and design through an earthly ungodly monarch, what can He do through a believing heart? God uses wind, rain, storm and any other part of creation to complete His designs. Water will freely mix with water, as oil will mix with oil because of the oneness of their nature. So the Almighty is able to send to those who are of the same nature as the Lord. It should be our nature to ask as it is God's nature to answer. It should be our nature to beg as it is God's nature to give.

When God supplies the need, you are dealing with the Owner of the universe, and it matters not to His nature whether to provide large or small, big or base. Margaret would soon realise that the Eternal is the Lord of the animal creation, including pigs, sheep, bread, honey, fruit, eggs, hens and all that is in the world. When He supplies the need felt in a desire He sells one of His many sheep, pigs, lambs. Each part of creation is a deposit of the glory of God, Romans 1:20. He owns the cattle on a thousand hills, yet it was not the hills that were required nor even the cattle, but something from a pig. God could send a pig farmer to her and meet the need with ham that was fresh off the bone and a fresh product of a whispered prayer? If God can, God will, and if God will, God can.

Earlier in her ministry, while pioneering a church in Gainsborough, Lincolnshire, England, God had sent a farmer with lots of vegetables (pressed down, shaken together and running over) when there had been a need. All Margaret had was meat, she lacked the vegetables, and the Lord sent them fresh from the fields. Could He, would He do it again?

Margaret was thinking that if the ham had been supplied the eggs could be added, and that would make a fine meal. The ham was the sacrifice, and the eggs would be the offering. The ham had cost the pig its life; while the hen could live on to lay more eggs.

Putting these thoughts of ham to the back of her mind, she was prepared to accept that the Lord knew what she desired, and there was the faith that the Lord of 'all things' could supply 'all things', and what she had desired was one of those 'all things' are yours.'

Approximately two days later, Margaret had forgotten about the incident, having left it with the Lord. Her son Marcus came home from work. Marcus worked for a national company that had a strong policy on food and employees consuming it or taking it home. They would rather feed the food to rats or put it into the incinerator, but they never gave any away. Their profits were in food, and the food was to be cooked into money in the restaurant. So when he returned from work with a package in his hand and a smile as broad as the horizon on his face, Margaret wondered what it was as he presented the package to her as a challenge to ask the question, 'What is that you have in your hand?' The impossible and the improbable had happened.

The place where he worked had given him one pre-packed ham that was as large as it was red. It would fill the frying pan. To Margaret here was that 'pressed down, shaken together and running over' the sides of the pan. All she had to do was to add eggs, and the desire she had a few days earlier would be satisfied with such an abundance that could only come from an assurance of a prayer answered and a need met.

As those smells wafted around the kitchen, each one was the smell of a prayer answered and a need met when humanly speaking the need could not be met. When one door closes, God opens another four. When we reach the place of accepting what we can't obtain, God sees that it becomes ours, not in short or small measure but so much more than we have anticipated. This became an encouragement to her faith in a Lord who interprets our desires, and sees those desires met with His fullness. It is the desire to grow that turns the acorn into an oak tree.

Please note: the prayer was answered, the need met, but Margaret had to do her part in obtaining the frying pan, and putting heat under it. The Provider did not turn the ham over in the pan when one side was cooked. God did the supplying and she did the frying! God did the sending and she did the receiving. Good things come in large parcels as well as small. Here was much from little, that little being a desire for a slice of ham. With a little more faith a pig might have appeared on the front lawn!

As Margaret received the ham, a sense of the love and compassion of God filled her being which was stronger than the smell of ham or eggs. That food would soon disappear before a healthy appetite, but in God it was something that would outlast all these things. The fragrance of God's unique presence filled her spirit. This was much more significant than the ham and eggs in the pan. Saying grace over the meal that day meant more than usual, for in a unique way the Lord had provided this wonderful meal.

23

THE OPEN ALTAR

Margaret had gone to visit her sister Hilary who lived in West Yorkshire, England. They were so close as sisters that in everything they did they were like twins! The church they were at seemed too small for the numbers attending. The people were like the animals going into Noah's ark before the judgement of the flood. Each person seemed to know where to sit, and where to go as they entered the building. It was as if they were following a Shepherd who was leading them to the place of pasture, pleasure and the land of plenty. How green would the grass be this morning? Would this be the time of still waters and overflowing cups? The minister preached the word of God, not as a loaf of the Bread of Life, but piece by piece so they might understand all that the Lord had to say. The minister understood that little birds or chicks must have the food broken in order for them to swallow. These children of the Lord as they received the word of God would grow in the nurture and admonition of the Lord, Ephesians 6:4.

He was pleading that the lost would be found, the empty would be filled and the broken would be healed so that they would serve a useful purpose in the community. The theme of his message was taken from Jesus looking over Jerusalem, and weeping because they would not come to God, Matthew 23:37.

The prayer he offered was that they would become useful to the Master, and not become as ornaments or items in a museum. The theme of his message was 'Hearing the voice of the Spirit; being aware of God's visitation.' There was a holy hush as he rose to his feet, as if he was the Prime Minister making a keynote speech to a packed House of Parliament.

With strong passion the minister was trying to persuade the people to surrender. As he spoke, he opened so many doors for them to come back to the Lord. He spoke as if he had limited time, and he mentioned that the people had a limited opportunity to do what the Lord was asking, seeking and demanding of them. He told them, to emphasise what he had to say, that 'opportunity' for the Greeks was a man with a bald head with a tuft of hair on the front, the rest of the head had been greased, so if you missed the tuft as the front you had no chance of taking hold of the back of the head as your hand just slipped over it and you were left grasping thin air!

These people came to church but were not in favour of full surrender because of the cost. To surrender to the Saviour of the soul would hurt as much as putting your hand into an open fire. The reserve of the people must be removed. The sovereign grace of the Lord must abound on the right and on the left.

Many felt that their best day had gone. The sun had set whilst it was day, Jeremiah 15:9. What light had been theirs had been snatched away, leaving them in the blackness of outer darkness. Would they never be able to succeed? Would they ever serve again in the white hot of zeal for the Lord? The hand that had been wide open on the cross had slowly closed, and they were left looking at a fist that threatened judgement.

As Margaret listened to the preacher, the sky opened up before her, and she saw the heavens opened but no dove descended, Matthew 3:16. She wasn't in the church at all; she was in a totally different place. No wonder the children of Israel had longed for the songs of Zion, Psalm 137:1–3 while in strange circumstances and captivity. The Lord was revealing to her things through the Spirit, which appeared as a film shown on a screen.

There appeared an open altar with large flames rising up from the base. It was the shape of the altars in the Old Testament, but it was not made out of rock, as taken from a mountain side. This altar had been carved out of the love and mercy of the Lord. Each curve and pattern was lovingly shaped to perfection.

The writing was embossed, making it stand out on the altar. It was placed where nothing would impede anyone wanting to make a sacrifice. There was no hedge to leap over, no bridge to cross. The altar had been deliberately put into an open area so that no one might be hindered when approaching it. The fences had been removed. In the Old Testament there were people who had to keep the road clear that led to the City of Refuge, Numbers 35. John Baptist prepared the way of the Lord, Mark 1:3.

This altar was not as the one that Moses built with the tabernacle with a fence around it. That was an emblem of the law, but this altar represented the grace of God without fence or door. It was as wide open and as accessible as the heart of the Eternal. The altar measured 18 inches wide and 24 inches deep. It was a small area that held burning coals of fire, as that which Isaiah saw in Isaiah 6:6. The fire was in the altar and the altar was in the fire. It was devotion as represented in the fire that would receive what they had not given. When fire burns it makes us willing to move because the flames are hot. Whatever the people offered, the fire converted into its own likeness and nature.

The Lord wanted them to be as a flame of fire

held in an altar, but converging on and converting everything they came into contact with. They could be as a flame of fire in an Ice Age, and in a dark world fire could show the way to a better day. As this picture stood out from anything else in the church, so they could stand out and be a revelation, a picture of God in the poverty and pollution that surrounded them. The flames of the fire could become spears of flame that would penetrate and overcome other weapons of warfare. These flames would be as tongues of fire as seen in Acts 2:3.

It was a small altar, but it contained the fire they required. There was no reserve in this altar. Every part of it burned with fire as the bush did in Exodus 3:2–4. A small heart, if surrendered to Jehovah, would be filled with so much fire, fire that burns, fire that liberates, fire that shows the way, fire that results in sacrifice. Whatever the people offered would be matched by the fire of the Lord. It would remove all dross, and turn silver and gold into that which is purified seven times.

They would be as fingers of fire that point the way to the Lord. As every spark and flame was in that altar so the plan of God for each life was represented in a flame. When we reveal zeal that is part of His zeal, then all will be well. They could burn with passion in Him. They could be what they were always intended to be in this fire.

The fire was so bright and intense that Margaret

was looking for Elijah and Mount Carmel, but both were missing, 1 Kings 17. This picture was dedicated to fire. It was not the altar that was important but the fire of God that burned in it. While the people surrendered to the Almighty the fire would burn brightly. What had almost gone into smoking flax had now become a flaming fire, Matthew 12:20. Without devotion, without fire, we get taken up with the altar and what the Lord demands. With surrender we get taken up with devotion as seen in these flames. Then the emphasis changes, it is not what the Eternal demands but what I can give, pressed down, shaken together and running over.

Margaret noticed that there were no ashes, no clinkers in this fire. This was pure Pentecostal fire seen in the shape of flames that could burn and sever, melt and mould, shape and cause anyone to acknowledge His lordship over us, and to exalt Him in worship. The priest need not rake out the ashes. There were no carnal clinkers here. Each sacrifice offered became part of the fire. The fire decided what it would become and where it would fit. That which was large could and would be made small enough to fit into the plan of God. Anything misshaped could be changed into the shape required. That small would be made as tall as the flames as they ascended heavenward on an unalterable course. These flames were missionaries of devotion. The fire, by implanting its own nature within them, would use the usable and unsuitable. The talent long buried would be unearthed in the fire that burned. The more the sacrifice offered, the more the hungry flames rose up heavenward, as hands of flame that were worshipping the God of fire. This fire was hungrier than hunger, more desirous than desire. These people had what the fire wanted. There was in them that which would satisfy the will of the Lord. We often think and speak about our zeal for the Lord, but what about the Lord's zeal for us? What is zeal but devotion with clothes on? We think of our devotion to Him but what about His devotion to us that follows us all the days of our life?

The altar was filled with the fire of God, holy fire that was different from any other fire. The glory of God had been turned into flaming fire, the flames leaping higher and higher as if trying to reach the sky and melt the sun, moon and stars. As each person came to offer sacrifice, the fire flamed higher, and what they offered was immediately converted into sweet smelling incense. This fragrance as if from a shattered vase of aromatic oil filled the whole house. The smell of the fragrance was greater than the heat of the flames.

This was fire that purified, fire that took the objectionable and the obnoxious and turned it into something fragrant as saffron. As the people came to offer their lives as a sacrifice, they were immediately arrested by the aroma coming from the fire. Their lungs began to expand as they breathed deeply. This aroma was heightening their love for the Almighty. They had never seen fire like this, had never smelled the smell of His garments of aloes, myrrh and cassia before, Psalm 45:8, but now they wanted more and more.

The more people came to the altar the brighter the fire burned as if it was hungry for the sacrifices of the people. As each one surrendered to the Lord, the fire flamed higher and higher, yet they were not burned up as Nebuchadnezzar's men had been in the fiery furnace, Daniel 3:22. They were warmed as some of the warmth of the flames entered into their hearts. It was good for them to be in this place. Certain perfumes are only released by crushing and heating.

Whatever the people brought would be filled with this fire. Those things in their lives needed to be enlarged, shaped into the shape of God. Lives became flaming altars as rich and red as seraphim or cherubim. That gift given to the Almighty would be acceptable, would become as the altar that was already surrendered to the fire of God. This was a day of fullness and burning, receiving and blessing. What the people possessed had lacked fire; what they surrendered would have fire within, around, underneath and above. They could only crown Jesus with many crowns when they had a crown of fire. These surrendered soldiers would become 'one holy flame', not just 'tongues of fire' but flames of fire burning, consuming all as a greedy pack of wolves. The hunger of the fire would enter into the people as they surrendered what they had to the Lord. What they lacked the fire possessed and would possess them, so that their dark night would be illuminated. That given in surrender would not be lost, but it would be added to. The spark could become a flame.

The more the people sacrificed, the greater the fire flamed. The more they gave, the sweeter and more profound was the smell of the incense. God was telling them that the day of opportunity had not passed by. It would be there as long as the fire burned. They had to show commitment to the purposes of God by holding nothing back. They had to be as greedy to give to God as the flames were hungry to burn up what was offered. The requirement was to have hearts as an open altar, and then the fire of God would visit the church.

If they held back that which was demanded by God then the fire would cease burning, the altar would disappear, and the day of opportunity would be removed. The altar of stone would be just stone, as empty as an oyster without a pearl within. It would be the fire that would add lustre to their living and be the plan for the church. When you gaze into an open fire, you can see a thousand shapes suggesting something different, so from these scared flames many forms would come forth as brands plucked from the burning lit by love. This fire was creative, and in it were a thousand possibilities for each life. Their lives would be as the fire with a thousand missions, a thousand messages, a thousand shapes and sizes with suggestions that come from flames of fire. Others could be lit from their fire. From a small spark a whole prairie can be made to burn.

The altar, the fire and their response would meet together, and would be a light that would never go out. This move would be more than Mount Sinai belching out fire and smoke. It would achieve more than past history diminishing into something of historic value.

This was no 'lake of fire', it was rather a lake of love as seen in the fire. The love of God was as red as the flames that greedily licked up the gifts that people were giving. As they gave, whatever was being held back could be set free as a rope being burned in the fire, and allowing the prisoner to walk free. The increase was in giving to the Eternal, the loss was in holding back, and tending to poverty, the poverty of not having a heart filled with zeal.

This church had a choice of an empty, burned out altar or one filled with flaming fire. That fire would meet every need for it would burn up what was offered, but would also attract others, who would want to see why it burned so brightly. The brightness of the fire, the burning of zeal would be witnessed as the people surrendered. The more they surrendered the more zeal would be exhibited in the form, force and fullness of fire. The new life would be as a red flame of fire. They would become soldiers dressed in red. Theirs was to be another Pentecost as the God of Elijah heard their cry, and made them fit to live or die.

There would be nothing cold, religious or formalistic about this church. Its designation would be one of fire, fire that burns brightly, fire that all could see where they were going wrong and how to put things right. It would be the fire in the altar that would show the people what they were withholding and what they should surrender as coals to a fire. In the light of His revelation the deepest needs would be met. If you put your hand with a steel glove on it into a roaring fire, as you take hold of that fire (or try to), whatever you seek to take does not diminish that flaming torch. Grace given remains the same forever as long as there is fuel enough.

As this prophecy was given by Margaret, people commenced pouring out to the front of the church. They came stampeding because they had smelled what they were hungry for. Some were weeping, some were quietly moaning, as a prisoner is pronounced guilty, and is about to be sentenced. This was the source of deep devotion that they were being invited to, where glory-fire would become healing-fire.

The words that came to the people as they merged at the front of the church were 'See us on Thy altar lay, our all this very day, to crown the offering now we pray, send the fire.' 'God of Elijah hear our cry; make us fit to live or die, to crown the offering now we pray send the fire.' No one can tie a flame in knots; even attempting such a thing will cause them to be badly burned. This fire was not for burning it was for blessing. That day the people of God were blessed as they were touched afresh by the fire that comes from the Eternal.

24

MAPLE SYRUP

This was to be a remarkable visit to Canada for we were to visit a Baptist church in Picton, Ontario. On a recent visit one of the leaders had said we had 'funny accents'! My reply to that was it was not us that had a different accent but them! This visit would certainly be different because we wondered how they would accept the Lord speaking to them through the gifts of the Holy Spirit. As Jesus went before the disciples into Galilee, so He had gone before us into Canada to prepare the way.

Canadians are sometimes more British than the British with many of them displaying the Union Jack from flagpoles in the gardens or from their front lawns. They speak so highly of the Royal Family and the United Kingdom. When they mentioned the Queen it was with devotion and a tremor in the voice rarely heard in England's green and pleasant land. They spoke as if they had a paying interest in the House of Windsor, and would certainly have made great ambassadors for the United Kingdom!

It was April 1996, a day that was to be a red letter day, when God would speak to hearts and lives. What Margaret prophesied to the people of Canada was long before the outpouring of the Spirit took place. Many went from Canada to take the 'maple syrup' to other nations. Very few evangelists had ever gone from Canada to be an ambassador to the world at large.

We had been invited to speak to hungry people who wanted to be filled to overflowing. The people were as lively in the Holy Spirit as those Hebrew daughters that had children born to them, and had been so active at birth that the children had been born before the midwives arrived, Exodus 1:19. These people had a deep hunger for the Lord.

We needn't have been afraid or suspicious about our reception because we discovered that the same zeal throughout the world for the Name of Jesus Christ was in these Canadians who loved to worship the Lord. Their worship was loud and long, and always expressed in song. On that Easter Sunday morning you could see a swathe of colour as ladies danced before the Lord, waving banners high and low. There was a dimension of the Spirit in this church that could not be measured. This was a Pentecostal Baptist church, where fire and water readily mixed together.

As the service began with a song and a prayer, the Lord began to move from seat to seat, aisle to aisle and person to person. People were being physically and emotionally moved by the workings of the Holy Spirit. The response of those who had gathered was jubilant, as if welcoming home a victorious army and 'VE' Day had been declared. Their exuberance was ecstatic; their worship came from the offering of body, soul and spirit. There was the constant rhythm of the Spirit of God moving as notes from trumpets, harp and dulcimer and other instruments until the whole became an orchestra of oneness praising God.

There was not one ounce of discouragement in the place. Not one flicker of a fading light was seen. If the pulpit could have raised itself in worship it would have done so. They felt they had something to sing, shout and dance about. They danced in ever increasing circles of love and faith. An unseen choreography was at work as everything was done decently and in order — the order of the Holy Spirit beating out time from the heart of God.

Someone here had lit a fire in their hearts which was burning brightly. These believers wanted, needed and reached out for God as those being rescued from deep waters reach for the hand of the rescuer.

Margaret began to feel a surging, which she knew was a sign of the activity of the Holy Spirit.

It was as if she was standing under Niagara Falls. Wave after wave passed over her until she felt like Moses whose name means 'drawn from many water', waters that did not take her under but over and on into the sea of blue before her that was a shadow of heaven. There was so much power rising and falling through her body that it was with difficulty that she stood. There was the feeling of being a cork in the water and as a ship passed by the cork was just being tossed backwards, forwards, downwards and upwards. This did not make her seasick; it was for cleansing and restoring. Using what the Lord was doing, and holding on to His word as a strong fence, she was able to keep on her feet to speak out to the nation of Canada.

The words that were prophesied were not given in any picture form. The words that came from Margaret's heart came directly from the Lord. She was the conduit through which the Holy Spirit flowed. As the Lord poured in so she poured out. These were words that were framed in the Holy Ghost, full and forceful, pure and sure. They had the 'ring of truth' about them. They could release burdens and lift up that laid low into a strong position. She was the mouthpiece of the Lord, although she might have felt like Moses who said he could not speak. With the mighty power coursing around her spirit she could do no better thing than to tell what the Lord had told her. That received in secret was going to be published from the housetops. She had something to tell, and Someone to help her to tell.

It was the time of sap gathering from the maple tree, in order to turn it into syrup. Outside of farms and houses you saw many were advertising the syrup that they had taken from the maple tree. This syrup was so good that the maple leaf became the emblem of Canada, appearing on the national flag. There were many promises offered with the syrup. Good health, good eyesight, good muscles, everything except life or the mouth to eat it with.

Margaret was proclaiming that a king or ruler was about to enter the building, but in this case it was the King of kings and Lord of lords. It was the same call and conviction of the trumpet being sounded to gather for battle to rout the enemy. That given to Margaret was so bold it seemed as she spoke as if a torrent of water had been released as seen in the word Perazin, meaning 'The god of the Breakthrough'. The modern translation of Isaiah was seen in action. 'When the enemy comes in, like a flood the Spirit of the Lord will raise up a standard against him', Isaiah 59:19.

The Canadians knew their seasons, knew the difference between winter, summer, spring and fall. These people knew the difference between chalk and cheese! Cheese tastes better to them than chalk! As nature ran its course, so the inhabitants of this land responded to the things that nature was saying, and as the trees and the contour changed colour, so they responded to the time of the year and the time of the day. They knew when it would be hot or cold or even both on the same day, and because they knew they made provision. They knew when it was a time to gather, and a time to sow, described in Ecclesiastes 3 where it says 'there is a time'. The winter would soon be upon them, freezing everything in its icy grip.

They were trusting in a natural process as sap became syrup. This given to them from the Lord would mean that they needed to depend on the Lord for their future prosperity. God must become the Tree, more than the family tree. The Eternal would stand with more arms of comfort and love than the branches, leaves, or even the number of maple trees that had ever grown in this glorious place called Canada. God's salvation was sweeter than maple syrup.

'You as a people have gone to the maple tree for your syrup. Knowing it is time you go there and every year you return to retain that most needed and sweet to the taste. You know what is required is not in the bark, branch or leaf of the tree. As you have come to the maple tree for syrup, so the time has come for this nation to come to God. In Him is that outlasting anything gathered as fruit from any tree in the world. Your future is not in a tree or in its sweetness but in tasting and

seeing that the Lord is good, Psalm 34:8. Now is the time to come to the Almighty because He has been storing up that required by you as a nation. The new shall flow from the cross of Christ. God wants to heap into your bosom so that it is pressed down, shaken together and running over. This that the Lord wants to give you has no measure, it is without measured capacity.

'That which is used to gather the syrup is small, and can only contain so much. Here is the promise of much more! You come with your containers, but He longs to give you that which cannot be measured by mug or jug.

'That given by the Lord will not run into emptiness, but into fullness that helps it to keep its capacity. He is not calling you to come and go, but to come and come until your cup is full and running over. When it runs over He will pour in even more of His abundance, for His nature is the nature of abundance. When He counts the apples or the fruit on any other tree, or even sheep in the field, He never stops counting because what He creates keeps coming, keeps appearing as if it is being born at that moment for that purpose.

'As you come to the Lord, your capacity to receive and give will be increased, in fact of the increase of what He does there will be no end. This supply is not as small as your gods; it is as large as the heart of God. No one individual or church will be able to take all that is given. That is why

it will include your sons and your daughters, and this nation of Canada. The supply is so great and the tree is as large as its source that whosoever will may come and taste of the sweetness of His salvation. The relishing is in the tasting. The asking comes from the receiving that will lead to tasting.

'That which you receive will be so plentiful it will be exported. That given by the Lord in Canada will be exported over the seas even as maple syrup is. The evidences of revival shall go from this country throughout the world. It will commence as sap in the tree, but will develop into something larger until all the containers in the world will not be able to contain it. It is for sharing, it is for caring, it is for giving.

'This move of God will be better than a bumper year in syrup services or Maple mercies. You will export what has been given to you so that this nation will become famous not for its military prowess, or its maritime fleet but for revival power. You as a people will be in that power, and as you enter into it you will take and use it for the healing of the nations.'

As this power swept the place men became like drunks. With their eyes closed some were swaying backwards and forwards as if they in the breeze. Others were bent double or on knees with hands raised as if they were touching heaven on earth.

The Canadian believers were dependant trees.

The sap of the maple trees was taken and by a process turned into sweet tasting syrup. It reminded us of the British firm Tate and Lyle who on the front of their tins of golden syrup had a quote from the Bible: 'Out of the eater came forth meat, and out of the strong came forth sweetness,' Judges 14:14. These words were spoken by Samson to describe the honey found in the carcase of the lion. Each temptation that comes to us as a roaring lion, if torn apart, if conquered can release a new sweetness into our disposition. What the world finds empty and tossed on one side the Lord takes and fills with the freshness from heaven.

On returning home to the United Kingdom, the newscaster stated that in Canada it had been such a bumper year where the sap of the maple tree had been turned into syrup, that thousands of cans of maple syrup had been exported throughout the world. What had been achieved in the natural would take place in the spiritual, and was already happening. As we flew out of Canada, the maple syrup was flying with us back to the United Kingdom.

Since that day a number of revivals have sprung up in Canada, and the sweet content of it has been exported throughout the world. Men of God have gone from Canada to promote the glory of God in other nations, bringing many, not to a maple tree but to the cross of our Lord Jesus Christ.

25

MANIPULATION

There were times when a minister or his wife would ask Margaret if she would seek the Lord and bring an answer to a particular problem. The answer was never the problem, but within the problem was the answer. Every problem is a golden opportunity to seek and know what the Almighty has to say. What the Lord says has a beautiful way of re-creating chaos into cosmos, Genesis1:2–4. A difficulty, although twisting this way and that, can be the straight road to the throne of God. Long before a problem becomes an argument we need that given by God that settles all matters of conscience and conflict. What the Lord gives is like Jesus putting calm into a raging sea, taking the wind out of the storm and speaking peace, so that we travel in peace rather than in the boat tossed to and fro by waves (see The Message Bible translation of Mark 4: 39). The answers given were always better and more available than the problem. Problems are forgotten when the answers come. In the birth of a child the pain of the birthing is forgotten.

One minister's wife asked Margaret if she would seek the Lord and bring her a word for her husband. God never stops at one, He has many sheep and all are in need of a shepherd. When the sheep wander it becomes a problem. The wool can get into our thinking. The open mouth of the wolf can be mistaken for the green grass browned by the scorching sun.

Seeking the Lord in the night watches Margaret never failed to receive something. That given was as scent, as ointment and a balm, for the grace received could be applied to all with diseases. The mind of the Lord can turn matters into multitudes of blessings.

On other occasions, when Margaret met with individuals or couples, she would feel there was a problem in a marriage or in a church or even in some other relationship. When this happened, she would take the problem to the Answer. That problem can be as heavy as a mountain, but through prayer can be ground into dust that blows away on the wind. The answers received were as outstanding as they were correct.

While in Ontario, Canada, Margaret was introduced to a man who was a distant relative of David Livingstone, the missionary to Africa.

After meeting him and his wife, Margaret felt that there was a 'thorn in the flesh' in their relationship. There was a tension so great it could have been cut with a knife and was without measure. Things that she did not understand were always taken to the One who understands all, creates all and answers all if we will call on His Name. When we go into the presence of the Eternal with a handful of mud, we discover the gems that are in that mud as we pray. Good things come out, for all things work together for good to those who believe, Romans 8:28. Telling the Lord is to allow Him to weave together all the broken strands until one whole glorious pattern is seen. 'Bad things happen to good people.' The reversal also is true 'Good things happen to bad people.' When Margaret received the bad as a bad apple, she simply removed the seeds, and sowed them into a promise with the prayer that they would re-appear as good, wholesome fruit.

Being on itinerant ministry there was not a lot of time in the day to seek the Lord, so when lights were turned low, Margaret began to seek the Light that never fades with the day.

When earth's day finishes, heavens new day can open up in the heart. Going to the Lord for Margaret was like going to a treasure trove, an Aladdin's cave, with such rare contents to be seen. Whatever was needed would come as silver and gold in the spiritual realm.

Paul and Paula were both strong characters and a pack of wild horses would not have held them back. They were filled with vision and a strong love for Jesus Christ. Zeal without knowledge can lead to fanaticism. Knowledge without zeal can lead to formalism. Both these believers had a ministry and both wanted to go and to get for God.

Sometimes complementary ministries can become competitive. It is only when we feel secure in what we are doing that competition dies a death. One should have been encouraging the other instead of pulling in the opposite direction, their attitude towards each other describes the word 'doubt' in the New Testament, meaning 'to be pulled two ways', Matthew 21:21. This is what causes a split. We cannot be as a boat pulling out to sea with one foot in the boat and the other on dry land! The description of the word 'contention' (Jeremiah 12:5, meaning 'to fret, going backwards and forwards like a saw blade'), is seen in the circus actor that rides two horses at once. It is easy when both are travelling the same way, but beyond the impossible to control when travelling in opposite directions. 1 Thessalonians 2:2, the meaning of 'contention' is 'fight'. These two are aptly described in these words.

Paula was always being held back, hauled back and put into her place of submission. Like a fish in the hand, she slithered this way and that, and it was almost impossible to control her. There was a need for her to be found sitting at the feet of Jesus, Mark 5:15, and in her right mind, then other things would never disturb her peace.

Margaret felt that the Lord must be sought on this matter, so she began to pray. The first person she saw in her prayers as the Spirit of God descended as the Revelator was the minister standing by a wide stream with a fishing rod in his hand and a look of pleasure on his face. His face was weather beaten, where the sun had kissed it many times. He had the look that every fisherman has when he is telling you about the one that got away! Don't think it is just fishermen who exaggerate, ask a jogger how many miles they jogged this morning! Ask a mountaineer how many mountains he has conquered. Ask the lone golfer how many holes he has achieved in one shot.

The fishing rod was bending and Paul was struggling. What was on the end of the rod? Was it the depth of the water that was causing him to strain? Was it an old boot filled with icy water or a bicycle on the end of his rod? Maybe he had caught a whale or hooked a treasure chest?

Paul was really struggling, but the strange thing was nothing was coming to land. He seemed to get whatever was on the end of the hook to the side, took a peep at it, and then let the reel free until the line went out into the depths again. This seemed to be a strange way of fishing, fishing never to catch anything. It was as bad as the disciples who toiled all night and took nothing, Luke 5:5. If this continued all day then Paul would have to invent many stories, stories even greater than the moon being made out of green cheese or boys being made out of snails and puppy dogs tails!

With real zest Paul was bringing the line in again, hook, line and sinker with something on the end that he did not want to catch, only to keep control of. He repeated the actions five or six times, sweating profusely. Would there be no end to this aborted mission? Margaret couldn't see any fish in his keep-net; in fact he did not have one. This seemed to be a favourite place and pass time for Paul. He was in his element; he had been created for this purpose and hour. This was his chief ministry of letting the line go into the deep just as far as he wanted it to go, and then to wind in to where he first cast the line into the water. There were fish large and small in this river; why, oh why, didn't he catch even one? Here was Jonah but where was the whale?

Paul continued with this religion of letting the line run freely for a time, and then bringing it back to where he was without revealing what was on the end of it. The man obviously had a secret that he wanted to keep from every other fisherman. If it was kept under the water then he could pretend it was anything from a whale to buried treasure that had been brought to the surface. What was his dark secret? What was on the hook at the end of the line? Maybe he required the same power that raised the axe head from the waters as found in the story of Elisha? 2 Kings 6:5–7. Maybe if Jesus could have told him to cast a line into the waters a fish would come to the end of the line with a coin in its mouth? Matthew 17:27.

The Spirit of the Lord was revealing to this praying woman that there were other intentions in Paul's heart than fishing or messing about on the river. The line was coming in again after it had been let go into the deep waters. The ceremony had been just about completed when Margaret saw it was Paul's intent to bring whatever was on the end of the line and caught on the hook to the place by his feet, as any fisherman would bring a fish.

Margaret did not know what to expect! The suspense was tangible. Slowly the line came in with a float and a hook. He was not being made 'a fisher of men'. Slowly first one thing began to appear and then another. Was it? Wasn't it? A thousand shapes seemed to pass through Margaret's mind as she watched this man in action.

She was disappointed because on the end of the line was a silvery fish that seemed so small in comparison to her expectation. All that going in and out for one little fish? It was like a long story with a small happening at the end. What did all this mean?

The Lord began to tell Margaret that this was a

picture of the relationship between the man and his wife. His wife, Paula, was the fish on the end of the line. That line was Paul controlling his wife, letting her go so far, but always keeping control of her.

The experience for this one fish taken from the lake was as bad as if demons were dragging her backwards into hell. The snatching of pearls hung around her ivory neck could not have brought a greater response. The frustration Paula felt when being let go and then dragged back against the current of the water was a hell made out of water! There was a boredom about it because after so many years she had got used to (rather was getting used to) being set free to be caged in by water. This lady had been set free but only so far as it suited her captor. Paula in the form of a fish had gone swimming for gold but only ever came back clutching the copper and zinc contained in the mud from the bottom of the river.

This was being tantalised, describing a Greek mythical person put into water up to his chin with fruit trees growing along the banks, and each piece of fruit coming near to the person in the water. The moment he went to drink or eat, the waters began to recede, and as he reached for a piece of fruit the branches were pulled in.

Margaret pleaded with the Lord to reveal more to her, for at the moment she only knew in part, and could only 'prophesy in part', 1 Corinthians

13:9. This was but a fragment of the whole story, just one episode. Margaret was as the apostle Paul wrote in 1 Corinthians 13:12, looking through a glass darkly — seeing things through water.

Paul was a man of dexterity when it came to fishing and bringing this person (fish) back from where it had been in the water. This was not giving someone enough rope to hang herself, it was giving enough line, and in time that on the end would come to its end where he was standing as a ruling monarch. 'Much practice makes perfect,' and this man was perfectly at home doing what he had been doing. He had done it all before, seen it all before, throughout the years. This line and hook was his control over those things around him.

What Margaret was seeing was unbelievable. The wriggling fish at the end of the line was the minister's wife Paula! Paula appeared on the surface of the water as a baby being born and forced into the world. The Lord needed to reveal to Margaret what it all meant.

The nearer to the shore Paula came, like a gigantic fish fighting for its life and supremacy, she was demonstrating her objections to what was happening. This was more than 'the battle of life,' it was 'life for a battle'.

Then Margaret understood. Here was a woman with a great vision who was full of enterprise. Nothing was too hard for her or the Lord. In her zeal she out-matched her husband. If it was deep she went to the depths. If it was wide, then she felt the call from the centre to the periphery. It was she who made suggestions when they were to be engaged in outreach ministry. When Paula stepped on to the water there was no thought of sinking, she was going to walk on water. This lady attempted so many things for God she was like a bold believer in the Acts of the Apostles in her outreach and adventuring nature.

Paul had a controlling nature, and every time his wife stepped over the side of the boat, he felt that he had to reel her back in. He felt threatened by her success. Whenever she suggested new things, Paula did them whatever he said, because she felt it was of the Lord; her husband — the villain of the piece — would bring her back to the side of the river.

Paula was a woman with a call that led to a collision course. The whole thing was a charade, because Paul was pretending to be a fisherman, yet under the guise of fishing he was controlling, revealing constantly that he was master and lord.

Even if the vision was of God this man must control all things. Paul thought that if he didn't they would control him. Paul would be pulled into the river, and he was no swimmer or fisherman, but he had certainly learned and mastered the art of control. He was not prepared to rescue his wife if she made a mess of things. This was his acumen, and he knew all about dexterity — 'the skill (the kill) of manipulation'. Watch anyone who claims they never control anybody. Sometimes they wrap themselves in the most colourful religious garment, and use such spiritual jargon, but inside they are ravening wolves wanting to control and to kill the spirit of adventure. If you deny something it does not mean it is not in existence. Deny the presence of Big Ben in London, England, but every quarter of an hour it will remind the world that it is still there. What we deny does not disappear. Paul would not give even an inch, but would allow enough slack only for Paula to reach out into the unknown depths when he could not determine where she was going, he would wind in the line, so that swimmer became a struggler.

His theology was wrong. He stood there as 'Moby Dick' with a minnow at the end of the line, yet fished as if the largest whale in the seas had entered into his river. Paula was treated as if she had trespassed by swimming in a river without a licence. Paul would determine depth, space, width and endeavour. It must be what he could control or understand, without it he was lost. The one that should have been a fisher of men became a lonely fisher of one woman. He was no 'kingfisher'! If he would have spent as much time seeking the lost in the highways and byways as he put into controlling his wife, then he would have built castles of grand accomplishment.

Taken up with controlling his wife, he had lost the sound of his call to the ministry. That ministry had been turned inwards, into his family, and he would not be bettered by this, but rather grow worse. The time he had spent in this river using his controlling spirit could have been spent as a pioneer, or as a missionary sailing the seven seas to embrace mankind with the love of God. If only he had faith to believe that raging storms could be calmed. He was the creator of storms but could not calm them.

Margaret confronted the couple when they requested advice, and told them what God had revealed to her spirit. The problem they came with was the one Margaret had seen in the Spirit. The man and his wife admitted that it was true to the finest detail. They asked Margaret to pray for them, and she did this using the knowledge that God had passed on to her to resolve this situation. The request was that their marriage would be healed, that neither water nor rocks would ruin them. As Margaret prayed for them she had the assurance that these two individuals became one in Christ Jesus. They entered into 'fellowship' — two fellows in the same ship, both on the same expedition and cruising as companions.

26

REVIVAL GROWTH

Tony and Teresa were a gifted couple who sought the Lord constantly. They sought to love Him with all their might, mind and muscle, in doing abundant works of faith. People stood back and inwardly applauded as they saw their zeal for the Lord. They had pastored one small church, and transformed it from a rabbit hutch into a sheep fold! When they accepted the pastorate there were few members, but through prayer, good works and hard work they saw a transformation in every department. They sowed, and reaped as they had sown. Their work was akin to the Roman Emperor who, describing his achievements said, 'I found Rome built on brick, and I left it on marble.'

The vision this couple had from God was translated into reality by preaching, visiting, praying, guiding and shepherding the flock of God. They found that their talents were unearthed where these people lived. They were so busy with 'this' and 'that' as they worked 'in' God, 'for' God, 'through' God and 'because' of God. Their goal was not converts or church buildings but God. If they achieved anything less than what they had been called to do, they would have considered themselves failures — square wheels on a cart!

The departments of the church were changed beyond recognition. The building was quite small, standing at the side of the road as you entered the village. The village mentality of the people had to be changed into a world vision. The light God had lit must not be in their small corner, it must go out into the whole world. They introduced a system whereby anyone out of work could find work. They had a department that dealt with Social Security benefits, advising as to the benefits they would be entitled to. If there were problems that needed sorting, or questions that needed answering, there was a department that could deal with those things. Classes were opened for the sick, needy and 'down and outs' to receive help when needed. All their endeavours were centred on Jesus Christ. Whatever advice was given and taken it always drew the person to Jesus Christ. The strings attached to all they did were the tassels on the garment that Jesus Christ wore.

They had a large family of sons and daughters, described in Psalm 127:5 as a quiver full of arrows. They began each day with a Bible reading and a word of prayer, that prayer was meant to sanctify any stray thoughts they had had during the night, ensuring their walk before the Lord in the coming day was sanctified. All of them submitted to the claims of Christ. For them to live meant Christ, they 'slept', 'thought', 'taught', 'breathed' and 'ate' Jesus Christ! Whether they attended school or were practising music in the church it was all Christ related. The family were a shining example of what a Christian family should be. However busy the parents were it did not stop them training their own family in the art of music, along with others who had any musical abilities. Each member of this Christian family was given work to do in the church. They pulled together as tractor and plough.

There had been an evangelistic campaign with a well known evangelist, and the results had been overwhelming. Men and women, boys and girls, were added to the church until there was hardly any seating capacity and people were having to stand. It was not a church for the young or old, but for everyone. Each meeting was alive with the exuberance of the Holy Spirit. If this was religion, it was religion set on fire. Every religious form and ceremony was tramsformed by the Holy Spirit until it became relevant.

Attending the meetings, you were amazed at the number of people who claimed to have received healing. There was no need to goad anyone, no one

296

was holding back. Different ones would stand and testify to what God had done in their lives. There was a 'buzz' about the place, as first this person and that one was engaged in ministry. Counting the adherents on one hand was gone; a calculator was needed to number the members!

The devotion of the parents travelled in many directions as they visited the newly converted. This new move continued for a time, and then things began to subside as if the tide had gone out and the sun had set.

Tony and Teresa decided, after such an exhausting time with this church full of new converts that it was time to move to another church. An invitation was received from one church that had been large and popular a few years earlier, but now had subsided into a smaller congregation.

They went for an interview with the Eldership but it did not go well. Things were said that made the Eldership decide not to invite this couple into the pastorate. The Eldership couldn't understand the vision of Tony and Teresa. Tony had spoken about knocking buildings down, and rebuilding, and this congregation, being older, had difficulties in accepting the changes that this would bring.

Frustrated, Tony and Teresa decided to let others know they were seeking to move into a new area, where a new challenge would sharpen their appetite for the things of God. They began to pray, and as they did so a door opened for them to accept another church in Manchester. The problem was that it was in one of the worst areas. It was so bad, so the locals said, that the birds did not sing, they just croaked! Dogs roamed the streets in packs belonging to no one. A number of families were claiming Social Security benefits; the average family had seven children and three dogs! In this area were muggings, lying, cheating, stealing, armed robbery, whoredom, and divorce, and that is describing the decent people! The church had known better days. The congregation consisted of about ten people, and Tony and Teresa with their family would be able to supplement the congregation. The church had prayed that such a couple would come to work with them in this needy area, and here was an answer to their prayers.

There were many problems associated with the church, as many as the pieces in a large puzzle! The couple were not informed, they simply went in at the deep end, and found the waters deeper than they had anticipated! They found themselves as non-swimmers in deep, dark waters full of crocodiles and other unmentionable creatures.

The building was large, and the few folk looked like seeds scattered in a flower box on a window ledge. To make it look more acceptable, they removed some of the chairs, bunched the people together in the meetings, making it look more like a sheep fold. The other problem was that these were bleating sheep with complaints about everything. The numbers were few, and the church administration had been deciding whether to close the church and sell the building. Tony and Teresa came to shepherd what seemed like goats! If it had not been for the intervention of a pioneer pastor, the church would have been closed, and become a statistic.

Tony and Teresa soon realised that the problems with the church outnumbered the congregation ten to one! If any more people left they would have to have a funeral. There were problems with the heating, seating, worshipping, and the outgoings were more than the finance that was coming in. This wasn't robbing Peter to pay Paul, both Peter and Paul had been robbed! Even the land the church was built on did not belong to the congregation. Tony and Teresa felt that it would have been better to pioneer a church rather than pastor these sheep mixed with goats and foxes!

The church had been well attended during earlier times, but because of disagreements, splits, differences of opinion and self willed people, it had decreased from an oak tree into an acorn. The church had gone downhill all the way, and this couple had arrived as it hit rock bottom. As the years passed the locust and the cankerworm had done their work. What could Tony and Teresa do but watch and pray?

Margaret Atkinson felt a strong urge to pray

for this couple and the situation they were in. She knew they were having more than just a jolt or a slight scrape, they were in something up to their necks, and could not swim through these difficult waters without help. This knowledge became a weapon to goad her to pray for them. Margaret decided to throw them a lifeline by praying specifically that the Lord would reach out His hand and remould the clay in this dismal, storm ridden area of Manchester. She believed the Lord had a design for this area, He loved these people as much as those living in affluent areas of the city, and in Margaret's mind was the fact that landscape artists take wasteland and landscape them until they are beautiful.

This was her prayer for the church: 'Lord, will You take hold of this situation, and turn it around to march in the direction that You decide. At this moment they are at the bottom of a hill, march them back up again, and let that hill be Calvary! This couple are frustrated, and need Your help. Let my prayer be an SOS for these in this dire situation. I know you have plans not to harm but to prosper. I don't know how you are going to do it, but reveal to me what you are going to do in this area. There are people in the homes surrounding that church who are naked, blind and rebellious. By your cross, wipe it all away, and bring them into the house of the Lord.'

A few weeks later Margaret, along with Terry

her husband, had to meet with Tony and Teresa. It was not going to be a meeting where pleasantries were exchanged, then everything forgotten, so that nobody reveals how they are feeling. It would have been so easy to ask 'How are you?' 'Oh, I am fine, thank you' — then to move into small talk about the children and family, which would have been so unrewarding. When you meet with people who are suffering, it is so easy for them to put a religious smock or coat on, and cover their deep feelings. From a distance a weed can be mistaken for a flower, but one lacks beauty and scent.

This was to be a meeting of discovery and revelation, because as Margaret had been in prayer, the Lord had been speaking about the church and these workers. Margaret had a message from the Lord. The plans had been laid in Margaret's heart, and now they were about to be revealed.

When they met, pleasantries were exchanged. The usual, traditional thing. How are you? How are things going? Are the family alright? To every question there was a stock answer, but it did not reveal the heart, the hurt, the frustration of God's lambs. Then Tony and Teresa began to let their heart overflow in their conversation. They had much to tell, grief upon grief about this difficult, impossible work they were engaged in. They no longer had the same command or helpers that they had experienced in the former church. They felt they had made a mistake when accepting an invitation to pastor this church. They began to form a list of the things that were wrong in the area that was so negative, and if it had been a sunny day so far, the clouds of despondency, doubt and fear began to gather.

Manchester is known for its rainy climate, but as these two spoke, problem after problem began to rain down as to why the Lord could never do anything in this place. Tony and Teresa had drunk deeply at the waters of discouragement, and only the wine of the kingdom could alter the situation. This couple had been cast adrift from what had happened in their previous church. There had been as many problems there as here, but those problems had been of a different nature. This couple had become so discouraged that yellow was made out to be pink, and blue became black, red became dark green, and everything was mixed in their conversation. They were transported into captivity, the seventy years of captivity Israel had suffered and, as they spoke, it was as if the opening chapters of Ezra or Nehemiah were being read. In these was the Book of Lamentations without its consolations! Torn down walls, houses devastated, place ruined, and hope disappearing. As the darkness deepened we were in the three hundred dark years without any revelation that is between the Old and the New Testament.

Margaret broke the chain of events by looking at them both, and beginning to tell them as she prophesied what the Almighty was going to do in their area, and with this church. The words were powerful and began to wrench the unbelief out of the heart of the couple. As she began telling them what the Lord had told her, their faces screwed up, and it looked as if their eyes were being closed to the revelation, as if they could not bear to look at the vision presented. They were hearing about the glory of God, and instead of taking their shoes from off their feet as Moses did, they were placing hands over their eyes. It was Abraham who was told to look and see the land before him, and look towards heaven with the look of faith, Genesis 13:14. The way they were looking was not the look of faith, but the look of doubt and fear. How could God take this situation and turn it around?

They gave Margaret the blank stare of the man who cannot believe in miracles. We were reminded of the blind man Jesus touched who could only see men walking as trees, Mark 8:24. They had suffered so much; they could hardly believe what they were being told. It was like prisoners being told of a paradise island that they would be released to. They didn't seem to welcome wholeheartedly what the Lord was going to do. They had suffered, and it had closed their hearts to what the Lord was able to do.

Margaret was saying, 'Where the flock has been small, it will grow into a crowd of worshippers that adore their God. There will not be room in the building that you are in to contain what God is going to do. That building will have to be extended. There is going to be a revival here. You will not have to look to the north, south, east or west, because it will be where you are. You have limited the Lord. When you should have been swimming in the sea, you have carried a glass jar with water in it, and that has satisfied your spirit. It has seemed destitute where you are. The Lord will bring people to you, as He did before, because your church has had an illustrious history, and history will be repeated on a grand scale. The barren will sing because of the children that will be born. She who is called barren and is rejected shall be accepted with a large family. The Lord is going to send a revival here that will be a revival of growth, praise, witnessing and praying. The Lord is going to increase what you have if only you will be faithful.'

We must now go forward a number of years to that same church in the same area of Manchester. Now the birds seem to sing. There is a different spirit in the church, that which was desert has blossomed as a rose. There is a sense of destiny as you drive into the car park, facing a well maintained and freshly painted building that cries out 'Look, they all love me!' There is a notice board on the wall of the building proclaiming the activities of the church. As you read, you wonder how they have time to breathe! The highway to

God's city runs through here. You have to arrive early to obtain a seat in the church. The inside of the building has been renovated and is delightful. The music is good, and the congregation has greatly increased.

It is a joy to be there, the joy of the angels is shared as sinners come to repentance. A lot of hard work has been put into this place to transform what was a shell into a place that has soft lights, good music, and great times of worship. They have plans for bigger and better things. The word spoken by Margaret a few years earlier have been fulfilled, every jot and promise, bringing to remembrance the time Jacob called a certain place 'Bethel', the house of God, Genesis 28:19. From the stone that he used for a pillow to rest his weary head, revelation after revelation changed that one stone into something else. It was there the anointing flowed, as he poured oil on the rocky pillow. The presence of God was felt for he testified, 'God was in this place and I knew it not.' It was the doorway to heaven with angels ascending and descending!

The sparse has become plenty as the church goes from strength to strength. God saw what Tony and Teresa could never see, and did what they could never do. The glory of the Lord is in this church as they feast on the finest of the promises of the Lord. The church is a picture of inspiration and dedication, as one cannot do enough for the other, but all want to do everything with all their might for the Lord.

All this happened when Tony and Teresa had left the church. They did not stay there until God fulfilled that promised through Margaret. They only think of what might have been if they had stayed the course and obtained the prize. It has been left for another to complete the course and obtain the promise.

27

DOORSTEP EVANGELISM

It was one of those October days where grey clouds lingered for ever. It was the season between summer and Christmas where joy would have been a welcome guest, and the silliest of jokes would linger in the memory long into the deep winter days. The garden had ceased to blossom, the leaves were beginning to fall, flowers were going to seed, and it felt as if the bloom of youth was diminishing. Something unusual was called for that would split the sides of this dark, dismal day into laughter.

A burly man was standing at the small blue gate which led to the side door of the house. Margaret noticed that he was frantically waving his arms about like a wind turbine, and she could not tell whether he was in distress or was simply trying to attract her attention. He began to point towards the side of the house where our little, harmless dog was tethered. Margaret could not hear what he was saying, but something was obviously causing him concern. Then he shouted. 'It is the dog!' pointing at it with his forefinger. Margaret looked around for a vicious dog, thinking that one had strayed into the garden, then, on realising that he meant our six inch high dog with its placid temperament, she began to smile and assure him 'The dog will not hurt you; it is called 'Tiger' but names can be deceiving,' she said, as she removed the dog from the pathway. The man would not accept her word, for previously a dog had bitten him, and he had found its bite was worse than its bark! The man replied, 'You see, Mrs., I have been bitten by a fierce dog, and I am afraid of them.' 'Well this little dog will not bite you,' said Margaret as she sought as a nurse to assure the patient that all would be well. 'The dog bit me in the leg, and I am still in pain although the bite has been treated.' He exaggerated his limp, emphasising his pain, as he told the story of the dog bite. To her it seemed as if the cat was afraid of a mouse, or an eagle was fearful of a sparrow, for our dog was small and this man was large. Margaret continued to assure him that everything was alright, but he still would not come near the dog.

The man was from a courier firm to deliver one of the many parcels that come to our home on a regular basis. The man with a large face had timidity written over it, although it seemed misplaced because he was such a robust man. Margaret had never met a trembling giant before! He continued the conversation, 'I was bitten by a dog, and my leg is still so sore that I can hardly lift the parcels, and it has made me so afraid of dogs.' As he said this he began to run his hand up and down his leg gently as if not to disturb any lurking pain.

Margaret said to the delivery man 'Can I pray for you; God can heal your leg.' He looked stunned, as for a brief second all conversation ceased, as if a truce had been called, then, with a bewildered look on his face, said, 'I will go and fetch your parcel!' This strong man could handle large heavy parcels, small letters and all manner of objects in packages, but had difficulty in handling prayer, a woman praying for him, and the name of Jesus. He ambled away to his van and returned with the parcel huffing and puffing as he placed it on the floor. As Margaret signed his pad as proof of delivery, he began to mention his sore leg again, as if he was constantly reminded of the dog bite. He didn't want to forget what had happened to him, so to keep him wary of dogs he continued to mention it. 'This left leg is still in such a lot of pain, and I can assure you dog's teeth are like razors, they sear through the flesh. It was like being attacked by a shark!' Margaret thought to herself, 'That's a bit of exaggeration.' Even if he could forget, the pain served as a sharp reminder of a previous battle of man and dog. Man's best friend became this man's enemy because he had been bitten by a dog!

He had the wounds to prove what he believed. When he returned to the depot with undelivered parcels, he had an excuse as to why they could not be delivered. The word 'dog' was written under the name and address!

So Margaret continued, 'I can pray for you if you wish.' He paused for a moment, collecting his thoughts, trying to make them fit into his picture of thinking, trying to work out what this would mean, then he replied 'Okay, I don't suppose it can do any harm.' When he said this it sounded like the last words of a man in a sinking ship. There was doubt in his words as to whether God would hear this prayer or answer; such a thing as prayer had never entered into his heart. Prayer was a virgin thing to his manner of life and conduct, something his wife did not pack into his sandwiches when he was about to leave for work! This was something that was not on his work sheet for that day! He had met with many things such as biting, chasing, snarling dogs, complaining people whose parcels were always late, because some wanted them delivering the day before they were posted! He had even been threatened, but not with prayer!

Then he bowed his head with a forlorn look on his face as if he was surrendering to something he knew nothing about. For him it was like a lamb going to the slaughter. Whichever way he turned he could not win, for this woman was very persuasive. If a woman believed it, then how could he as a man not accept it! Margaret began to pray for him, with the sky above as a cathedral roof, and the wilting flowers as a congregation. The quiet, yet authorative voice sounded out over the garden, as if it had been the Garden of Eden and this was the cool of the day in which the Lord would speak to this Adam. 'Dear Lord Jesus, heal this man from this dog bite. Remove the pain from his leg. Make this leg as whole as the other, and cause him to know that he has been healed. I ask you this, the God of mercy, in the Name of Jesus.'

The delivery man looked up, as if he had been a school boy in an assembly, and with a look of surprise on his face he began to stamp his leg on the floor as if he was a marching soldier. Then he began to slap his leg with a bemused look on his face as if he could not believe that he had been prayed for on a doorstep, and that the pain had gone! The picture he presented was one etched in amazement. As he demonstrated his healing, he was muttering certain undetectable words over and over, but Margaret was sure that he wasn't swearing, praying or giving God the glory! She could not interpret his mumbles, not knowing whether he was praising or complaining! Was he saying it was a good thing or a bad thing?

He had approached the house in fear, but he

left it with a different kind of fear, the fear of the Lord which is the beginning of wisdom, Proverbs 9:10. He knew that something had happened; he had something different in his life that was not there when he commenced his shift that morning. A new day had broken. He did not want to wait to find out the answers to his questions, because when this woman prayed he did not know what would happen next!

It seemed strange to him that a woman he had met on the doorstep had not been talking about the Manchester weather! A woman had hit him with the full force of religion. His work friends would never believe what had happened to him on this October day that was turned back into summer through the prayer of a woman. He could now be assigned to heavier parcel delivery. He went towards the gate with a spring in his step, as if he had a breakfast of spring lamb! With a look of wonder and amazement and amusement on his face. What he had found this morning was not on his navigation system!

The delivery man had delivered his parcel, and Margaret had seen the man delivered. They had equally done what they had to do in obedience, the man to his employer, Margaret to her Master. While Margaret was signing for the parcel, the Lord was putting his signature on a man's life in the form of healing.

There was the familiar sound of the door bell

ringing. We were tired of the constant telephone calls and the sound of the door bell, in fact life seemed to oscillate between these two things, mostly time-wasters clamouring for attention and money, wasting God's precious gift of time to our lives. The dog was barking above the noise of the doorbell.

Whenever people rang the door bell, from Jehovah's Witnesses to Mormons and postman or milkman they were entering into 'perilous times'. Margaret made it her business to pray for them whatever the need was. She would stand there with two hands outstretched as if they were branches from the Vine. As she reached out to touch others, she was plucking brands from the burning. Her hands were her two evangelists reaching out for the lost.

Margaret in her daily meditation had read in the King James Version of the Bible: Exodus 37:18 –21, where the word 'out' is used five times relating to the work of the candlestick of light filled with oil, which died as it brought light to those in darkness as the oil and wick diminished. The branches went 'out' of the side of the golden candlestick. The light shone 'out' from it. It was never meant to be an internal thing. What God had given Margaret was for those outside who were looking in. The best way to keep what you have is to give it away. Evangelism had to start somewhere, why not on her doorstep? Why must it always be on the street that others live on, or on a doorstep belonging to another? World evangelism commenced on Margaret's doorstep! Why not use your own doorstep as a pulpit? Other houses are visited in evangelism. Why not your own?

Two young handsome men stood on the doorstep. They were well dressed, not a bit like vagabonds or any one trying to steal while the door was open. They looked a picture of health but not wealth as the story they told would reveal. Margaret was never threatened by the stranger at the door, because she knew that some entertain angels unawares, but she wanted to be aware of what the Lord was doing. Every opportunity must be taken and used for 'the night would come when no man could work'.

These young men had not just arrived, they had been sent by the Lord. Margaret saw everything in these terms: 'All things work together for good to them that love God,' Romans 8:28. God's purposes would be fulfilled, whether the circumstances were 'good', 'grey', 'sad' or 'bad'.

The thought, on seeing them, would cross your mind that these were Mormon missionaries. Margaret asked what they wanted. She always disarmed people by calling everybody 'love'. They began to explain the reason for their call.

'We are students,' the bolder of the two commenced, 'I am trying to get back to Israel, and my friend is trying to get back to Holland. We are hoping to raise the finances to get back to our own countries.' Their plea for assistance was in their faces. They sounded rather pitiful as they gave their explanation. They reminded Margaret of two straying sheep that had lost the shepherd.

'We have this album of pictures, you can have them framed, and we wondered if you would like to buy one? Can I show you some of the pictures?' He pulled a thick album from under his arm, and proceeded to offer it to her. Margaret took the album, and flicked through the pages. Were they the drawings and paintings of these two young artists? They were photographs of difference scenes and people. There were a number of attractive pictures that she might have bought. Then she noticed one of a nude woman, and she said to the two young students, 'I couldn't buy that one, it is so rude! I am a Christian, and I love the Lord Jesus Christ. How much are your pictures?' 'They are £30.00 each!' With a sharp intake of breath, Margaret said to them 'That is far too dear; I could not afford to buy one at that price.'

The young men looked disappointed when Margaret said she could not afford one of the photographs. Then she added, 'I can pray for you!' This took the young men completely by surprise. They were open young men and they raised no objection to being prayed for, although they certainly had never had this offer before when selling pictures or doing anything else. They thought you could only be prayed for in a church or a synagogue!

The young men looked towards her, and she took hold of their hands, as if her arms were the branches from the Vine, and these two young men were fruit that was to be attached to it. She began to pray to the Lord. 'Dear Lord and Saviour of mankind, I bring these two young men that need you. May the Holy Ghost come upon them from this day! Make a way for them to travel safely to the country of their birth, and when they arrive there make them conscious of You and your reality. I pray that they might come to know You as their Saviour.' As she prayed the Kingdom of God was being expanded, and two young salesmen were being challenged by the Holy Spirit to surrender their lives to the Lord. As she did her part the Holy Spirit did His work on these young hearts. More quickly than they had approached the locked door, the Holy Spirit descended on them, and they began to blush, as something began to move on them.

They had never been prayed for like this, had never felt like this before. This was something from another world that they knew nothing of. In their heart the question was being asked as this woman prayed: 'How can these things be?' Little did they realise that Margaret was quoting from God's photograph album, the Bible. Her prayer for them came from her heart not from a glossy photograph. If you expect the impossible try the improbable, was a motto of Margaret's. If you go out on a limb, at the end of the branch you will find Jesus Christ with His hands filled with fruit. To the atheist, God is nowhere, but Margaret had a different interpretation of those words, and they are, God is 'now' 'here' as she fervently prayed for these young men.

As she finished praying, she let go of the hands of the young men, and looked at them, and their eyes were filled with tears; they were close to weeping. There was a longing in their faces to know more about this God that the lady had prayed to. They moved away from the door full of thought, inspiration and humility. Something had been developed in them which was more than a photograph. Margaret's prayer was that the nature of Jesus would be developed in them after they had repented and believed on Jesus Christ.

28

FREE MUSIC LESSONS

We had served as ministers at a church on the outskirts of Manchester for seven years, and were to stay as ministers for a further three years. The area was a mixture of rich and poor, old and new. The church was well attended, and among the adherents was a small family of mother and two daughters, Anne and Lorraine. Lorraine appeared much older than her age and consequently as a minor needed protection from older men who appeared as men with a wolf's nature. The daughters attended the church on a regular basis, whilst their mother came occasionally.

The younger sister, Anne, approached Margaret with a request for prayer for her family, who were in great need. Her father was an alcoholic, her mother was suffering from cancer, and her sister needed the Lord's protection, because she constantly got herself into dire situations, described not as 'hot water' but 'boiling'. As she approached Margaret, she said, 'Margaret, will you pray for my family, my mum and dad, and my sister?' 'Of course I will,' Margaret replied. 'Now what do you want me to pray about?' 'Please pray that my dad will be delivered, and my mum will be set free from cancer, (and this appeared to be so important to the young girl) because her hair is falling out due to cancer treatment, and I used to love to run my fingers through her hair and comb it, even sometimes plaiting it for her.'

Who could deny a plea like this from this young girl with soft eyes that pleaded as if they were dogs begging for scraps? The mother, Joyce, used to have beautiful red hair, now it was like string. 'Let me hold your hands.' The two hands reached out to clasp Margaret's as they prayed together. Here was the young and not so young joined in making a covenant with the Lord, and agreeing together about hurt. God would not deny these a listening ear or a loving heart. After Margaret had ceased praying, Anne lifted her head. Margaret let go of her hands, and their eyes met in unison of purpose. They felt that the Lord had heard their prayer and would answer.

As they were about to part, Margaret felt urged of the Holy Spirit to ask Anne about her own needs. Once you have prayed for others, then you can pray for yourself. The butter that has been spread on your bread, tasting nice on the slice, can also be spread on other slices. 'Anne, is there something that you would like the Lord to do for you? Have you any dreams that you want the Lord to fulfil,' asked Margaret. 'Are there any promises that the Lord has given you that have yet to be fulfilled?' Anne had made a decision to follow the Lord a couple of years earlier, and had grown in many areas of Christian life. Now, as they sat on a park bench in town, God would teach this young woman a lesson, and He would also teach Margaret a lesson. God's lessons are not found in an exercise book or written with chalk on a blackboard. They are of the occasion of the heart. God's schoolrooms are in nature, in a park, or in a shopping mall.

Anne, bowing her head, said to Margaret, 'I feel that the Lord has been working on my heart, in fact He has been working overtime telling me what He wants me to do in life.' Margaret lowered her head as she listened, wanting to catch every word that was so precious in the sight of the Lord. Margaret listened intently, as if an important announcement was being made on national news, knowing that if you gave time to others, they would give time to you. If you listened to them, God will listen to you, for the law of repeated blessings was in operation. 'I think the Lord has told me that He wants me to learn to play music,' Anne said, and then hesitated as if she had told a lie, and wanted to catch the words back into her mouth. Margaret had never been aware of any musical ability in Anne. Margaret herself was a musician, often playing the piano and organ in the home and in the church.

As if she hadn't quite caught what had been said, Margaret bowed her head a little closer to the young mouth, Anne then repeated what she had said, and, as if to emphasise it, Margaret repeated the words. 'I want to be a musician for Jesus. I want to be part of God's sympathy in symphony.'

'We can certainly pray that the God who inspired the Psalms, who has inspired so many songs to His glory, and who loves us to praise Him with musical instruments, will answer your prayer. You see, Anne, God by His Spirit places things into our hearts that He wants us to do. They are birthed in our hearts as we begin to pray. Prayer is the first step to God granting what you desire.' Margaret began to point out a few more scriptures to encourage Anne to believe that what was in her heart had been placed there by God, who placed the stars in the sky.

Margaret prayed a prayer of passion. 'Dear God You are the interpreter the deepest desires in our hearts. Let this young woman find a keyboard and put her hands on the notes to play the music of the heavenly sphere unto You. There may be difficulty in making payment for these lessons, but where the difficulty is, sound a trumpet, and let that lead the way into your will.' The young girl managed to mumble a few words and, being mixed with faith, God would sort out the mumble and jumble, turning it into musical notes and a musical instrument that would be worthy of any orchestral recital. The God who broke bread and multiplied it could, also, multiply these words into sweet music of the heart.

Whatever the weather on that Sunday afternoon had been, in their hearts it was now a sunny day and they had a sunny disposition. Margaret and Anne parted as friends with a burden for each other, which they would continue to pray about in future days. Margaret felt that musical tunes had already been deposited in this young heart by the Holy Spirit, for as they parted Anne began to hum a chorus she had learned in the church: 'Lord make me an instrument of worship, I lift up my hands in your name.'

A few days later Margaret was met by Anne whose face was beaming as if soaked in liquid sunshine. What a transformation from the dull face of a few Sundays previously when Anne had asked Margaret to pray with her. The prayer had surely been answered, but how or when Margaret did not know.

Anne began to tell Margaret the story of the answered prayer, and how God had intervened so that the prayer could be answered. 'When I left you the other Sunday, the words you prayed stayed with me. As I walked along I could still hear your voice ringing in my ears, compelling me to do things I would never do. Your prayer was being used by the Holy Spirit to direct my heart. As I walked along I kept saying 'Yes, that is right Lord, I want to learn to play a musical instrument then I can help others in the church to worship you.'

'As I went along the street near where I live, there was a plaque outside a house proclaiming the person living there taught music, I had never noticed the plaque before. It seemed as if the sun caught hold of it and the words written on it shone so brightly, "H. Henderson, Professor of Music, including Pianoforte".   I couldn't really understand what this meant, but something compelled me to knock on the door of the house.'

'Margaret, I felt fearful and tearful because you know that I am a little bit afraid, particularly when I have to walk alone. I gritted my teeth, somehow got hold of determination, and went to the front door and knocked. I seemed to knock so loud as if to shake the house down. I was afraid who or what might come to the door.'

'I waited a little while and knocked again. A man answered the door, filling the frame, a thin, tall man with spectacles up over his brow. He had a shiny bald head and he looked like a professor that I had seen in comic books and read about in girls' magazines. He reminded me of that seen in the film 'Goodbye, Mr Chips!'

The man cleared his throat and looked down over the top of his spectacles that he had let slip over his eyes. He said, 'Yes, what do you want?' Then, without waiting for a reply, continued, 'I hope you're not one of those silly children who find it amusing to knock on my door and run away, knowing I am too old to catch them!' I smiled at him through my fear, and the smile immediately removed any roughness from his voice, then in a silky smooth voice he said, 'Oh, I can see that you are not one of those, now what can I do for you, because I don't like my time to be wasted by vagrants?'

'I almost froze, because of what I was going to say next. In the background I could hear your voice and the prayer that you offered for me. At that moment a lark rose high in the sky over the park where we had prayed, singing as it soared. These two things were compelling me to stand my ground, and speak boldly to the music teacher, for that is what I thought he was. It was 'stranger than fiction' for me to speak to a stranger like this.'

'Then, just like a child stating the obvious, I said gently and a little fearfully, 'Do you give music lessons, sir? Do you teach piano lessons?' And then as if to put her off her mission, he pointed to the brass plaque and said, 'What does that say young miss?' At that moment Anne was wishing that a hole would open up in the pathway where she stood, and she could fall into it never to be seen again. She had gone so far but felt compelled to go all the way.

Then she spoke the unspeakable, and something you should never ever say to a teacher of music. 'You give music lessons, but do you give free music lessons?' The man was totally taken aback as if he had been a horse with bit in his mouth and somebody invisible had pulled on the bridle. He hesitated for a moment then chuckled, "Free piano lessons, I don't know of anyone who gives free music lessons! Do you think free music comes from my finger ends, young lady? I like your cheek, your style is out of the ordinary. Come in and let me talk to you, and see if we can come to some arrangements. Maybe your parents can stagger the payments."

'I was ushered into what seemed like a dream home, something like one of the 'Barratt houses'; I had seen pictures of their Premier Range. The walk from the front door to the living room seemed like a stretched eternity to me. It was as long as a boring mathematics lesson at school, where I used to scratch my head more than use my pen. As we entered the sitting room he said, 'Sit there. Now, what is it you asked me? Did I hear it right or did the falling rain affect my hearing, for it's not too good nowadays. You said "free" lessons?' And he emphasised the word "free" as if it was more important than any other word he had spoken that week. "Yes," I replied, "because we are a poor family."

'Then I began to tell him the story of my family with its sicknesses and the poor conditions that we lived in, including praying with Margaret Atkinson. I told him everything he wanted to know. I didn't have to think what to say, I just opened my mouth and said what was in my heart, as I felt inspiration take hold of my tongue. That day, in that room, I told the truth, the whole truth and nothing but the truth with the help of God. The music teacher listened intently without interrupting until I had completed my story. Then he swept his hand across his face as if he was trying to remove the wrinkles.'

'First I want to see if there is any music in you. Sit yourself comfortably on this piano stool, pull it forward, and use those magazines to sit on until you can reach the notes and pedals easily.' He opened a music book with drawings of animals over the notes. Then he began to show me how to finger the piano notes. He then asked me to play the scales, and left me there to practise what he had shown me, whilst he went to speak to somebody else in the next room.

'A few minutes later he returned. He had left so that I would not feel nervous, and also in order that he might listen to me playing from a distance, for that would give him a better idea of my potential as a musician, although at the time I didn't know this. "I can see and have heard that you have potential, and I like your audacity, so I will tell you what I am going to do." I half expected him to point to the door that would have opened of its own accord because this man had such authority. I remembered the words I had prayed with Margaret, that if two shall agree it shall be done. With a wry smile on his face he said, "I am going to give you free music lessons, you must come here every Tuesday at 4 p.m. straight after school. Now, young lady don't you dare let me down."

A frown appeared on what should have been a jubilant face after hearing what the man said. 'What is the matter with you now, isn't it good enough that I have told you there will be free music lessons; I thought you would have been hilarious with delight, but instead here you are frowning as if you are trying to crack your face!'

I began to cautiously say to the musician, 'I have another problem apart from not having any money.' Then Anne hesitated, as if the story must not be continued, as guilt arrested her in the middle of the conversation. 'I don't have a musical instrument!' There was a quietness rarer than a Sunday morning in the 1940s, that seemed to last for a long time but in reality it only lasted a few seconds while the music teacher re-arranged his brain cells. He wasn't used to this sort of thing, and

327

it had scattered his brain pattern, sending thoughts all over. He needed time to collect his thoughts. This young lady was so different, she was running him ragged! How could a child do this to him who was always in control, as in control as the piano note under the finger of a master musician? Then he said, as if this was his final word 'Alright, you can see that keyboard in the corner, I will bring it to where you live, and you can practise on it. Then I will have you come here each week to note your progress. I have never done this before, and I don't know why I am doing it. I hope all the street doesn't hear that I give free piano lessons, or else I shan't be able to keep the door closed or get into my own house because of the long queue.'

'He turned, took the keyboard from its stand, folded the stand, and went to fetch his car keys to take me and the keyboard to my home, so that my dream and prayer could be fulfilled. It was a large dream which had commenced by praying, then knocking on a door.'

Anne might have doubted that the Lord would answer her prayer, yet even when that prayer was answered, she was prepared to believe that God would stretch grace a little further to include a keyboard and a man who would deliver it to her house! She was prepare to believe one thing and, as she did, another prayer was included and answered. The Almighty loves ongoing faith in a child. The God who supplied the free lessons would freely give her everything needed to commence her training to become an accomplished musician.

Margaret had believed against all obstacles. To some it would appear that she had prayed an impossible prayer, yet that prayer had been prayed to God who takes hold of the impossible and makes it possible. We were reminded of this answer to prayer every time we heard Anne play her musical instrument or heard a band playing in that park on a Sunday afternoon.

29

MARCHING UP THE HILL

It isn't very wise or noble to leave the reader under a cloud in the last chapter of a book. I don't intend to do that. There may be clouds but I intend to leave you under the arch of the rainbow, where there is always the possibility of adding colour to your life and gaining buried treasure. I want to leave you gazing at the many colours of the rainbow, not the grey and white clouds.

When I wrote my first book *Paths of Righteousness in Psalm 23*, on the dedication page I wrote: 'Dedicated to my wife Margaret who has been with me through thick and thin, more thick than thin.' That is a summary of what is contained in this final chapter. I know that, 'the steps and stops of a good man are ordered by the Lord', Psalm 37:23 and Proverebs 16:9, but I also know that those steps can be up or down, very steep, and as slippery as a greased pole.

When Margaret began to swallow food it felt as if she was swallowing small pieces of glass. It was a cold winter's day when she developed a cough, and thinking it was just another cough I did not pay a lot of attention to it. The weather was quite cold in the winter of 2002. We did not know it then but it could have been our 'winter of discontent'. In these circumstances there was still the summer of contentment to be discovered. Like the apostle in prison we had to learn to be 'content' without letting the prison get into us, Philippians 4:11. We had to realise that whatever the situation, whichever way the wind blows, we are 'self sufficient' (Saviour sufficient) in Jesus Christ. Our sufficiency is in Christ, who is made unto us wisdom, righteousness and redemption, and 'all things' are ours, 1 Corinthians 1:30.

As the hours merged into days and weeks, the cough increased. It was a hard, harsh cough, and no matter how often Margaret coughed it was never productive. As the days passed by, Margaret grew weaker and weaker, in fact so weak that a kitten could have conquered her.

An appointment had been made to see the doctor. It is good to find out what is wrong with you, and then you can pray earnestly that God will heal you. Margaret and I have always believed in Jehovah Rophi — God the Healer. We had prayed for others and had seen God work miracles through those prayers. We knew Margaret was seriously sick when the pastoral leader from the local church telephoned, and as Margaret was talking, she felt herself passing out and fell backwards onto the bed.

The doctor suggested that a specialist should be consulted, and so on a cold February day Margaret visited the local hospital for a consultation. It was with feet heavy as lead that she went to the appointment. The symptoms led to the specialist to a solemn diagnosis, Margaret had cancer of the oesophagus, causing her to cough as her food passed into the stomach.

It might have seemed as if the light had been switched off, but somewhere in that darkness she saw the Light of Life. When you have been told that there is a cancer growing in your body, the promises of God take on a new meaning, and stretch high and low into whatever corner of life where there is faith. There can be that devilish temptation that God does not care. If He did, this would not have happened. The answer to those many temptations is: why shouldn't Christians suffer as the world suffers? Christianity will not exclude you from suffering. The hope, faith and peace in Christianity will give you the enabling power to accept and overcome. The silver lining in a cloud is faith in the living God. If a dark cloud comes to your life, look for the rainbow.

The specialist had confirmed that Margaret had a cancerous tumour of the oesophagus, but they were only his words and not the word of God. Margaret asked to be shown where it was in her body, and the specialist showed her on a computer screen. Gloom silently settled on the consulting room, but we were looking for the cloud of glory. Sadness was not allowed to be added to badness. The light in her life could not be switched on and switched off. It is at a time like this that you will see Jesus standing in the shadows. Jesus is the One who breaks the night with a new dawn.

After the hospital consultation, we were told that a further appointment would be sent through the post. We waited for a long time, but there was no communication from the hospital. When we enquired it was discovered that Margaret's case notes had been lost. It was only then that an appointment was made for her. The time of waiting was not wasted, however, it was used to pray and believe that, out of it all, God would reveal His purpose. At this time angels' wings would not have met the need, it had to be the hand of God filled with ointment stretching out to heal.

A decision had to be made. Should we trust God and leave it all with Him? Should we agree to an operation and still trust that the Lord would bring Margaret triumphantly through? God can heal by His word, by few or many. God has more instruments than any surgeon. The first thing we did was to pray, to look for daybreak and we did, Psalm 46:5 ('early' — before the dawn). Could we believe that dawn would break into the midnight hour? The Oversight of the church prayed for Margaret. People throughout this country and other nations were praying for her. More prayers were offered than the pain felt. Prayer went to the throne of grace from all quarters. People who had never prayed for the sick began to pray for Margaret.

On the Sunday morning Margaret, in accordance with Scripture, went forward for prayer and for the laying on of hands, James 5:14 and Mark 16:18. A number of Margaret's family with their grandchildren attended church for the first time in many years. The prayers offered were passionate, strong and bold; the ones who prayed meant to see the business of God carried forward on earth as it is in heaven. It was a morning of sunshine and tears, rainbows and clouds, pain and the promises of God offered freely.

The moment the news leaked out that Margaret had to have an operation to remove the cancer, people began to telephone. Margaret was in a weakened state because she could not take much food, and those who telephoned meant well, but some kept her on the telephone until she was almost fainting. Others decided to read long chapters of the Bible to her over the phone. One told her that 'this sickness is not unto death.' Others were passing on what they believed God had told them. 'All things work together for good to those who love God and are called according to His purposes,' Romans 8: 28. Yet some of these so-called helpers did not 'work together for good'. Lots of people said different things, but Margaret was not bettered by them but was rather made worse. In a strange sort of way they became Job's comforters, not that they spoke against Margaret but they give lots of detail without any substance. They quoted the word of Jehovah as if they were home bred, home fed and home taught parrots.

There are those thinkers (tinkers) who preach and teach that if you are not healed then there must be some sin in your life. They freely list seven reasons why you are sick. One is that you must be holding a grudge against another. I don't know how these peddlers manage when they get a common cold or an attack of hay fever or influenza!! All are forms of sickness. If it was true what was being said and taught, then we are healed by works, by what we do, and not by the Word of God or what the Almighty will do.

With these seven things in the life, a person goes to a meeting, and is gloriously healed. Was it because they had repented of some unknown sin? I don't think so; for they remained in the same condition they had always been in as they entered the meeting. They had believed the Lord all the time, but in the timing of the Lord there was a time to stretch out and heal, Acts 4:30. Why have some waited years for healing, and then suddenly they are healed? The conditions of both life and heart have remained the same. Healing is not based on a promise from the pages of a book; it comes from the power of God that was present to heal. The promises of the Lord are open doors for us to have our needs met. Revival is not based on repentance alone but on the sovereignty of the Almighty. Churches that are waiting for everybody to get right with God before revival comes are going to wait until the millennium!

Then there are those who come in 'unawares' (Greek sideways) who say you are not reading the Bible enough or seeking the face of the Lord. The Bible is the book that you lay your weary head on when you are sick. It is better than a pillow or a blanket. Those that are strong and well say you have no faith. Notice how negative it all is. I ask only one thing, if this is true what happens if none of those things applied to Margaret's life? We are then left in limbo; the silver tongue of the orator is made to stutter, to put his hand over his mouth. You don't have to be a dustbin to speak garbage. When Jesus raised a dead person to life, where was the faith of the dead person?

Someone needs to speak from the heart about the things that trouble them relative to suffering and sickness in the saints of God. If all the sick were healed, how would you rejoice with those who rejoice, but equally how would you weep with those who weep? Through the years of my pilgrimage I have seen many a Jacob who could wrestle with an angel of God, who could catch hold of his brother's heel at birth reduced to worshipping leaning on a staff because of old age, and to walk with a limp because the Lord has put something out of joint, Hebrews 11:21. I do not make the Lord the author of sickness, I believe it comes from Satan, but as with the trial of Job in the Book of Job, God has to give His permission, Job 1:12.

I am always amazed to hear how many folk who have never had sickness, and who were born with a strong constitution, put their good health down to their faith. Equally those who have and are suffering sickness blame no one but themselves, and some exponents of the word of God do not help them to believe. They will never bring you out into the sunshine of grace but will push you further into the corner until the corner becomes a hole that a mouse could go into.

A man may be seasick in a boat when the waves are choppy and the sea is rough. The boat is so small and the sea is large. That person will not be helped if you push the boat further into the sea, but they will be helped if you bring it into a haven or into port.

I read of Trophimus left at Miletus sick, 2 Timothy 4:20. I know of one with a thorn in the flesh and weak eyes. I know of believers who had had 'secret medical care'. There are those who believe you should always be well yet who have had operations for growths, and no one has known because they kept silent about the problem. Everyone who has ever lived and has been healed has ultimately died. Even King Hezekiah, having put the bunch of figs on his boil, still died when the time arrived.

I have written a book called *In Sickness and in Health* where some of these things are dealt with. On the back cover I ask a question: 'What happens if we do have faith, and in the natural process of time your eyes become weaker, your walk is a little unsteady, you find that memory is beginning to fail, as it lets you down again and again? Who will turn the sharp edge of the sword so that it is flat, and becomes a ceremonial sword rather than that which cuts into ribbons?' There is a need for compassion and grace in all of these things. Those who are sick will not be made well by being stabbed with a sword! Margaret must have an operation to save her life. The consolation was that her soul was saved, eternal life was hers.

Before the operation she had to go for chemo-therapy to shrink the tumour. During this period she had a 'stroke' down her left side. Then her body began to reject the morphine, and she began to hallucinate. That strong woman went back towards becoming one of Adam's ribs. It was a bad time, and the storm clouds gathered as much as they did in the days of Noah. Although the sea was raging around us we were in the boat with Jesus who seemed to be asleep on the pillow, Mark 4:38. When He left the pillow, He put Margaret's weary head on it as a place of peace and security in the storm she was passing through. That pillow became a pulpit preaching peace.

After many more examinations, explanations and deliberations the date was fixed for the operation to remove the cancerous tumour from her oesophagus. The dreaded day arrived and the operation was performed. It was a success but Margaret would never be the same again. They had cut away part of her food tract, and the two severed parts were joined together. The valve that prevented the food coming back into her throat had been removed. Every time she lay down there was the possibility of her food being regurgitated.

They had to enter the body at the side and at the back to carry out the operation, leaving a beautiful body badly scarred. After such an operation there is an immediate weight loss and bouts of sickness followed by diarrhoea on a regular basis. Margaret spent two weeks in intensive care — two weeks that were spent glorifying the Almighty.

Then the worst possible thing happened: the stitching where the two parts of her food tract had been sewn together burst open, and Margaret was bleeding to death internally. They had to operate on her immediately.

Margaret had a text on the shelf over the

fireplace which said, 'My assignment is greater than my attack!' On the crest of this card the words of William Carey were written 'Attempt great things for God, expect great things from God'. At the bottom of the card was the drawing of a cross, and reaching from the bottom the cross reached out from the words 'attempt great things for God,' to touch the previous words written in the middle of the card joining the words together. The word underlined: 'from' God. Then on the bottom the word 'for' God was underlined. The cross took central place in this design as it should in any life.

This is the kind of testimony Margaret maintained all the way through her suffering. You would never hear her complain. Things were done which you never thought a sick person would even think of, let alone accomplish. In her sickness she still ministered to and prayed for others. Margaret prayed 'touched with the feelings of their infirmities,' Hebrews 4:15.

The veil of suffering never blacked out the Lord, or drew a curtain over His face or features. If you listened at the bedroom door you would hear a sure and sweet voice pleading with the Lord to help her. Her prayers were her tears, not of suffering, but of joy and consolation. Every morning, when I walked into her bedroom, the Bible was spread out on her bed like an open altar or the two wings of an eagle about to take flight. Into a diary went the thoughts she had received the previous night or something that the Lord had deposited into her heart that morning. To Margaret this was manna from heaven, and must be gathered before the sun began to shine in its strength. This was her 'thought for the day', her 'word for today' that would be turned over in her mouth like a sweet when the pain increased in her suffering.

The Book of Job took on a literal meaning; that became part of her daily experience. It was lived as page after page in the home. It became more than something that happened many years ago to a man named Job. Margaret joined the family of Job. He became her father, brother and sister.

On other occasions Margaret would be at the computer, writing out sermon thoughts with the strong conviction that she would be able to preach the word of God again. These precious words were gathered as a farmer will gather seed corn for the coming spring. Each sermon was committed lovingly to a disc to be stored up for the day of release, the day of Jubilee.

Even in intensive care Margaret could not stop witnessing for the Lord. After being conscious for just a short period of time, Margaret noticed another woman who was in greater need than herself, so she called the nurse to her side. After anointing a 'face wipe' with oil, she asked the nurse to go and put it onto the other patient while she prayed. The nurse refused, because she said it would cause cross-infection!

While in hospital a friend called Sonja came to see Margaret, but this lady could not find the ward that Margaret was in, although it was only a small hospital. The lady was lost. Then Sonja saw a couple of women talking, and she stood listening. She thought she recognised one of the accents as being from her native country. When the conversation ceased, Sonja asked the lady if she knew the way to the ward where Margaret was. The lady knew the directions and gave them to her as readily as any fire will give warmth. This lady from a foreign country was far more congenial than a wooden signpost pointing the way to nowhere.

Before Sonja left, she asked the lady, politely, 'Have you been born again?' John 3:3. The woman was aghast, as if something had been said that had been brought from her past with a hammer blow. 'It is strange you should ask me that,' she said, 'I have been thinking that, I would like to know how to receive Jesus Christ as my Saviour and Lord.' That hospital corridor became a counselling room as two females stood together in a conversation that led to conviction. The woman was led to know the Lord, prayed for and given the address of the local church where she would find friendship and fellowship.

Margaret left the hospital in a weakened state. We began the customary rounds of seeing one specialist and then another. The circles seemed to get larger and larger, but no healing brought to the source. Every time we went, there was always the hope that we would find our utopia. The next visit would bring us to the panacea.

Before Margaret had her operation she was looking into a mirror in the kitchen that had been placed there, so if anyone walked into the kitchen quietly she would be able to see them. She gazed into the mirror; a shadowy figure was standing in the mirror. Satan began to speak to Margaret. With a triumphant voice, and a gleeful disposition, he said to her, 'I have now got you where I want you!' Every part of the shadow in the mirror could speak. The darkness of that shadow seemed to fill the room and everywhere she looked she could see part of the image of Satan.

Margaret's reply was swift and to the point. 'You may destroy my body, and part of me might have to be removed, but in my heart (she pointed to where her physical heart was) is God's salvation that you can never take.' Margaret knew the verse 'Greater is He that is within me than he that is in the world,' 1 John 4:4. 'I love Jesus,' and at the mention of His name the shadow disappeared and the mirror ceased to be a stage for evil. That photograph of evil had crumbled because of Christ. We must fear God and obey Him who can destroy both body and soul in hell.

These days Margaret does not speak publicly

as often as she did. Anyone who knows her may receive a telephone call from her to explain what the Lord is saying. Everything she passes on, there is usually a red ribbon wrapped around it as a token of his red blood and the peace of God. The days of despondency come and go, like autumn and winter, yet the Lord remains faithful. 'I will never leave you nor forsake you,' Hebrews 13:5, 6. Sometimes her sugar level falls dramatically and this weakens her, but that weakness never stops the prayers of God's saint ascending to the Lord. Life has been a struggle but in that struggle there has been a tighter grip taken on the things of God. Even when there has been the experience of 'free fall' we discover that the Lord is holding on even when we let go. You cannot fall lower than the Everlasting arms, and you can never drift beyond His contended care.

To add more thorns to the rose it was discovered also that Margaret had gallstones. The pain in her bladder would come across her stomach, tightening and squeezing the breath from her body. Added to this is the fact that she has constant bladder infections. In such suffering there is only one place to turn and only one Person to look to.

In 1940 during the Second World War, a soldier was severely wounded and needed immediate surgery. The only place that would be safe was the local church with its communion table. The table was at the far end of the church, beneath the figure of Jesus on a cross. As they operated on Tony, he turned to look at the cross, and as he did so it eased his pain to look upon the One who suffered such pain for us. Our suffering is only cheap wine while He drinks the dregs of vinegar found in pain. Greek liturgy, when expressing the suffering of Jesus, says 'Thine unknown sufferings'. It is through pain that God draws us aside, to what, sometimes seems to be a burning bush of pain. He speaks from that burning bush. That wounded soldier had only a statue to look upon; we have a living Christ who speaks in our pain. The pain did not seem as great while looking at the figure and passion of pain. Pain can be the pavilion in which we discover peace. Pain can be a shelter in a time of storm, but when you come to the shelter you will find Jesus in the shadows, not as a marble figure but as an ointment to ease the suffering. We may not know what the future holds, but we do know Who holds the future and all things by the word of His power.

Margaret is resigned because she is resting in the joy of the Name and nature of Jesus Christ for time and eternity. She knows that as she walks through this life holding His hands, one day those hands will gather her up, and she will be forever safe in the arms of Jesus. The Bible records that Abraham was 'gathered' unto his people like a flower gathered from a garden and taken into the gardener's house. Genesis 25:8, 17 describes sheep being gathered by the shepherd. Margaret will go into the bosom of Abraham, as a believer, Luke 16:22,23. That word 'bosom' describes a port where a ship comes for respite and refuelling, away from the wind and waves and into the quietness of tranquillity.